Foundations of Java for ABAP Programmers

Alistair Rooney

Apress®

Foundations of Java for ABAP Programmers

Copyright © 2006 by Alistair Rooney

Softcover re-print of the Hardcover 1st edition 2006

ISBN-13: 978-1-4842-2016-0

ISBN-10: 1-59059-625-0

Printed and bound in the United States of America 9 8 7 6 5 4 3 2 1

Lead Editor: Steve Anglin
Technical Reviewers: Gene Ames, Stefan Keuker
Editorial Board: Steve Anglin, Dan Appleman, Ewan Buckingham, Gary Cornell, Jason Gilmore,
　　Jonathan Hassell, Chris Mills, Dominic Shakeshaft, Jim Sumser
Project Manager: Richard Dal Porto
Copy Edit Manager: Nicole LeClerc
Copy Editor: Andy Carroll
Assistant Production Director: Kari Brooks-Copony
Production Editor: Janet Vail
Compositor: Dina Quan
Proofreader: April Eddy
Indexer: Toma Mulligan/Book Indexers
Artist: April Milne
Cover Designer: Kurt Krames
Manufacturing Director: Tom Debolski

Distributed to the book trade worldwide by Springer-Verlag New York, Inc., 233 Spring Street, 6th Floor, New York, NY 10013. Phone 1-800-SPRINGER, fax 201-348-4505, e-mail orders-ny@springer-sbm.com, or visit http://www.springeronline.com.

For information on translations, please contact Apress directly at 2560 Ninth Street, Suite 219, Berkeley, CA 94710. Phone 510-549-5930, fax 510-549-5939, e-mail info@apress.com, or visit http://www.apress.com.

The source code for this book is available to readers at http://www.apress.com in the Source Code section.

To Lisa, Samantha, & Justin.

Contents at a Glance

PART 1 ▪▪▪ Introducing Java

PART 2 ■■■ Enterprise Java

Contents

PART 1 ■■■ Introducing Java

PART 2 ▪▪▪ Enterprise Java

About the Author

ALISTAIR ROONEY has been developing software for over 23 years. He has been a programmer, team leader, project manager, and IT manager. Alistair started coding in COBOL and RPG on IBM mainframes and has coded in Basic, InfoBasic, Visual Basic, C++, C#, and naturally Java. Alistair spends his time consulting to corporations in the SAP arena. He teaches both ABAP and Java for SAP and other companies in Europe, the United States, and in South Africa where he lives with his wife and two children.

You will also find him developing and doing implementation support for various clients. He is a keen mountain biker during his time away from the office.

Acknowledgments

Thanks must go to Stuart Fripp for some of the ideas in this book, Steve Anglin for his expert eye, Stefan Keuker from SAP for his very sound technical advice, and Richard Dal Porto for bringing it all together. Thanks must also go to many of my clients for allowing me to experiment with their SAP systems, to SAP AG, SAP Belux, SAP UK, and SAP America for their guidance, and to my family for their patience.

Introduction

Java has been a part of developers' vocabularies since 1995. At first it was thought of as being a nice, neat little language that could do some amazing things for the Internet. However, the language soon matured, and it still kept its simple approach. Developers started to realize the awesome power of a clean uncluttered alternative to C/C++.

It wasn't long before visionaries in the industry discovered that Java could be further extended into an "enterprise" language. Thus J2EE (Java 2 Enterprise Edition) was born. This has also matured into a solid base for running three-tier, web-based, enterprise systems.

If anyone doubts the industrial strength of these systems, there are now a wealth of blue-chip corporations using J2EE. They use IBM WebSphere and other enterprise systems to create very large, robust, and "externalized" systems.

The dot-com boom may have adjusted itself somewhat, but it is by no means gone. The statement that the Gartner group made a few years ago, that corporations would have to externalize their data or lose out to competitors that have, is still very valid. Can you imagine working with a bank that did not offer online banking? They wouldn't survive for very long if their competitors were all "webified"!

So, in 2001, one of the most innovative ERP companies, SAP, saw an opportunity to bring Java into its development environment. SAP has said that Java and ABAP will coexist as development languages. With Web Application Server (WAS) 6.40, we have seen this become a reality. Although there is still room for improvement (isn't there always?) we now have a credible SAP platform for delivering web services.

Make no mistake—SAP is very serious about Java. It is not a passing fancy or an attempt to be fashionable. When I first lectured about Java to ABAP programmers in Europe in late 2002, SAP already had 35 internal projects using and developing Java. SAP has developed a "flavor" of J2EE to fit inside WAS.

In this Foundations book, we will be looking at the standard J2EE and the new Java EE 5. You will find it easy to use the SAP-specific APIs once you have mastered the standard version. Rest assured, though, that I will explain everything from an ABAP programmer's point of view. I will also show you the NetWeaver way where appropriate.

As I write this, Sun has recently renamed Java (Standard Edition) 1.5 to *Java 5*. Sun is also releasing Java 5 Enterprise Edition (Java EE 5), and this has been done as part of the Java Community process. This is important, because SAP (and others) have been part of this process.

WAS 6.40 does not currently use Java EE 5, but considering that technologies like Enterprise JavaBeans (EJB) 3.0 make life easier for developers, it's a certainty that SAP will include it soon. Rather than covering the old way of doing things, we will explore the latest technology so that you will be adequately armed for the next release.

Many books have leapt into discussions of how SAP employs Java *without* adequately explaining the basics. This book aims to reverse that trend by leading the reader through *bite-sized* lessons with *simple* examples that stress the points in the lessons.

Clearly, in my opinion, Java is a lot of fun. If you need an illustration of this, check out the Robocode project at `http://robocode.sourceforge.net/`.

I hope you enjoy this book. Remember to have fun with Java!

PART 1

∎∎∎

Introducing Java

In this first section, we will explore the basic constructs of the Java language. You shouldn't skip any of these lessons, since they will lay the foundation for the second part of the book. Always try what you have learned, even if it means copying the example code, as this will consolidate the principles in your mind.

■ ■ ■

Your First Java Program

Java is a funny language. The more you learn about it, the more you love it. The question is where to start to teach Java?

Java is a *fully object-oriented* (OO) language, and most people coming from an ABAP environment will not have had any real exposure to OO concepts. (Hands up if you have done the SAP BC401 course). OO is very important to Java, and most would say it's critical.

Normally I wouldn't talk about Java at all for the first few lectures in a Java course. I would talk about OO principles: inheritance, polymorphism, encapsulation, and the like. On the other hand, it's nice to see *some* Java to keep the excitement going.

The compromise that most lecturers come up with is to present a simple "Hello World" type of program, explore some OO basics, and then return to Java. That's what we'll do here.

Hello World of Abapers

Let's have a look at a simple ABAP program.

```
REPORT ztestacr.

DATA: v_hello(11) TYPE c VALUE 'Hello World',
      v_abapers(10) TYPE c VALUE 'of Abapers'.

START-OF-SELECTION.

    WRITE: /, v_hello, v_abapers.
```

What will this produce? A list dialog displaying "Hello World of Abapers".

Now let's look at the same thing in Java.

```java
class HelloAbapers
{
    public static void main(String args[])
    {
        System.out.println("Hello World of Abapers");
    }
}
```

That's it! That's your first program. Now we need to "activate" it, like we would activate the ABAP program, and the process in Java is somewhat similar. The Java program does not compile to native code but rather to *bytecode*, which is then interpreted by the Java Virtual Machine (JVM). (More about the JVM later in the book). To compile this program, we issue this command:

```
javac HelloAbapers.java
```

The file we've just written must be saved with a `.java` extension.

Figure 1-1 shows two separate examples of the compile command on the same screen: one with errors and then one with the errors corrected.

Figure 1-1. *Compiling with and then without errors*

Let's take a closer look at the Java code we've just written. The first line defines the *class*. As you can see, I haven't defined a variable for my string in this example. I'll explain why when we cover static variables.

Notice the curly brackets. This is how we define blocks in Java. They can be positioned anywhere, but it looks a lot neater if they are lined up and indented. The first curly bracket opens the class block.

The next line defines the *method* we are using. In this case, it's the main method. Every Java class that can be called or run directly from the command line must contain a main method.

Lastly there's the line that does the work. It calls a System object that contains a println method (I'll have more to say about the notation later). This method accepts a single parameter and prints it on the screen. The parameter is the string.

Don't worry at this early stage about the cryptic things like public or static or args[]. We'll cover those things as we go along.

Finally we need to run the program. If you try to run the class file by typing this,

```
java HelloAbapers
```

there is a good chance you will get an error similar to this:

```
Exception in thread "main" java.lang.NoClassDefFoundError: HelloAbapers
```

To prevent this from happening, we need to tell the Java runtime where to find the class file by providing a *class path*. In my computer, the class resides in C:\book, so I will inform the runtime by putting -cp in my command, followed by the actual path. As shown in Figure 1-2, on a command line I would merely type the following:

```
java -cp C:\book HelloAbapers
```

Figure 1-2. *Running our Java program*

That was easy, but obviously there is a bit more to Java than this. Stay tuned for the next lesson, where we'll start to explore the benefits of OO design and we'll look at what the various terms mean.

■ ■ ■

Object Orientation in a Nutshell

Help! I'm in a nutshell! What kind of nut has such a big nutshell? How did I get into this bloody great big nutshell?

Austin Powers

In this lesson we will explore the basics of object orientation. I will use a very contrived model to explain the basics of some of these concepts, and we will go into more detail in subsequent lessons.

The Nutshell—Encapsulation

Fantasize for a moment that you needed to speak to Bill Gates. Unless you're a bigwig in IT, the chances of you speaking directly to him are small. You will probably deal with one or many intermediaries. They will listen to your ideas and pass them on to Steve Ballmer who may not even pass them on to Bill.

That's how encapsulation works. You don't get direct access to the private data within a class. These are hidden from you. Don't feel offended—it's really for your own good. You need to use special methods to retrieve or change this data. Since the data cannot be changed directly, and can only be accessed through these methods, we can be confident that we have not changed the way the class works.

Now here's the bonus. We don't have to test the class or worry that it's doing what we want. It is a black box that we can trust will do the job. Java has a lot of these really neat classes available for use. They're called APIs (application programming interfaces), and they're kind of like super function modules. More about APIs later.

Figure 2-1 illustrates how classes function like nutshells. See how the private data is protected by the methods? In Java, we call these the *accessor* or *mutator* methods.

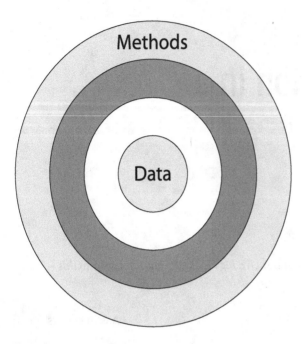

Figure 2-1. *The nutshell*

Inheritance and Polymorphism

Let's look at another concept within OO: inheritance.

Meet Joe Soap. He's an FI consultant, but he wants to go further. He wants to specialize in Treasury. So he does some extra training, becomes better at Treasury, and is now a more specialized consultant. Is he any less of an FI consultant? No, of course not. He still retains all that good experience he built up. Figure 2-2 shows this diagrammatically. We could say that the TR consultant is a more specialized FI consultant. We could also say that the TR consultant *inherits* all of the FI consultant's attributes and behaviors.

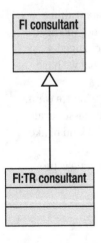

Figure 2-2. *A simple inheritance tree*

Let's consider a more accurate analogy now. Let's think about a shape. We don't know what kind of shape it is, but it has some attributes in common with all shapes. It has an area and it has a color. We can also give it a behavior. For example, a shape knows how to calculate its area.

Figure 2-3 illustrates this. Notice that the Shape class has two attributes and the one behavior. This is how we draw them in Unified Modeling Language (UML).

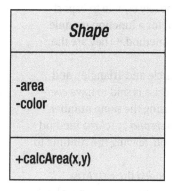

Figure 2-3. *Class diagram in UML*

This is where it gets interesting. We can now create three more specialized shapes that will inherit the attributes and behaviors from the Shape class, as shown in Figure 2-4. We call these subclasses. From their perspective, we call Shape the superclass.

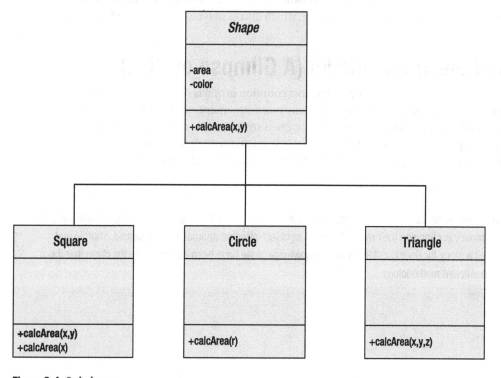

Figure 2-4. *Subclasses*

■**Note** Standard UML notation would not repeat any methods in a subclass. I have shown the area method again, in bold, in the subclass because I will add functionality to it. This repetition would not normally be done in UML.

The variables defined inside the parentheses in the behaviors loosely equate to exporting/importing parameters (depending where you look at them from) for a function module. Bear in mind that these are always the parameters being passed *to* a method. (They are the "message" in UML-speak.)

Notice that the parameters are different in two of the classes (Circle and Triangle), and they are the same for one of the methods in the Square. The Square class is said to have *overridden* the calcArea(x,y) method from the superclass because it is using the same number and type of parameters (or arguments). Notice that the Square has a *second* calcArea method with only one parameter. This is now *overloading* the calcArea method, leaving the runtime to choose the most appropriate version.

The other two classes, Circle and Triangle, are said to have *overloaded* the calcArea method and not overridden it, since the numbers of parameters do not match the superclass's definition.

To put it simply for now, the calcArea(x,y) method in Square (shown in bold in Figure 2-4) is the *only* method being overridden. Essentially, the difference is that the method *signature* is the same for the one method in Square and different for the others. This is the essence of polymorphism.

If this all seems a bit confusing, don't panic! I will cover this concept later in more detail. I'll also explain the concept of *late-binding*, which makes polymorphism powerful in Java.

The Conceptual Model (A Glimpse of UML)

I'm going to introduce you to one of the most common *artifacts* (the UML name for a document): the conceptual model. There are many more documents that can be used in OO design, and I *strongly* encourage you to do more research on the subject. It *will* make you a better Java programmer, and it will also enable you to write truly reusable code. (See http://uml.tutorials.trireme.com/uml_tutorial_navigation.htm for more information.)

■**Note** Several companies with the right resources have studied OO versus non-OO design before investing serious money in changing their methodology to an object-oriented approach. (For example, Sharble and Cohen did a study for Boeing in 1994.) To my knowledge, none have been able to refute the claim that it is a far more efficient methodology.

Let's take a look at a video store for an example. First we make a list of candidate classes, or concepts.

- Assistant

- Video

- Video catalogue

- Customer

- Video store

- Loan

There are a number of techniques that can be used to extract these candidates, but we won't cover them here.

We can now start to build associations between our classes. This will start to give us an indication of the responsibilities of each class, which is a very important aspect of OO design. Figure 2-5 illustrates this more fully.

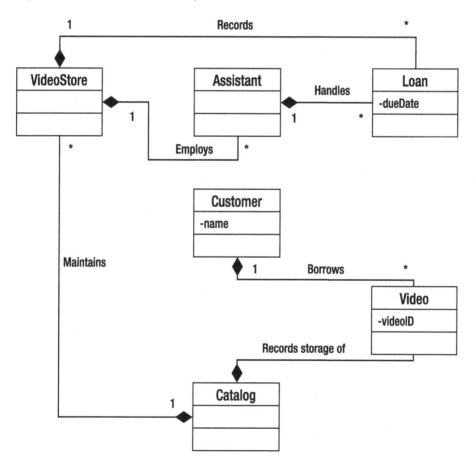

Figure 2-5. *UML diagramming*

Note Notice the numbering of the relationships. In Figure 2-5 we see both one-to-one and one-to-many relationships. The asterisk (*) denotes that there are "many."

That's a *very* brief introduction to the wonderful world of UML/OO. I've heard people say that it takes from six months to a year to convert a procedural programmer to an object-oriented programmer. You can only benefit from learning and applying OO principles, so stick with it! Personally I wouldn't put a time limit on it. It depends on how keen you are.

In Lesson 3 we'll explore some Java basics, such as the primitive data types.

■■■

The Primitive Data Types

Everything in Java is an *object*. You'll hear this refrain often enough on any Java course. And the exception to this rule is, of course, the primitive data types. I'll go through them quickly in this lesson, since you, as an ABAP programmer, will already have a very good understanding of data types.

Why do we have the data types we do in Java? Well when James Gosling (Java architect) started out writing the Java language, he likened it to moving apartments. He put everything (from C/C++, the *old* apartment) into boxes and then moved to the new apartment. He didn't unpack anything—he left everything in a box until he needed it, and then he pulled it out. After a year, everything that was left in the boxes was thrown out. It's not a completely accurate analogy but it is very close.

Boolean

This data type is named after George Boole (1815–64), the English mathematician who devised Boolean algebra.

Note The Boolean declaration starts with a small *b* as do all our primitive data types. Boolean with a capital *B* refers to the *wrapper class* and not to the *data type*.

The boolean can only have a value of true or false. It does not have a value of 1 or 0 and cannot be treated as such. Therefore you would test it like this:

```
boolean  a=false;
if (a = = true)
{
some code in here.
}
```

Note Because of the structure of Java syntax, you are not obliged to leave a space between the operator and the operand. In ABAP you must leave a space.

The double equals (==) tests a condition. The single equals (=) acts as an assignment operator (as it does in ABAP).

The default value for a boolean is always `false`.

Byte

In Java a byte is a signed, two's-complement quantity. If you missed the "what on earth is a two's complement value" lesson, please send an email and I will happily send you an explanation. Essentially it's an efficient way of storing negative numbers. A byte is 8 bits long and therefore can hold any value from –128 to 127 (2^8).

Beware of doing arithmetic using bytes. For instance, this code will generate an error:

```
byte a=10, b=20;

byte c=a+b;
```

Java always performs mathematical calculations at 32-bits precision, so you would need to *cast* the 32-bit answer into a byte to store the answer in c. We do this by placing the data type in brackets, like so:

```
byte c = (byte) (a+b);
```

Warning DANGER Will Robinson! There will, of course, always be a potential for data loss when casting from bigger to smaller data types. The *most significant bits* will be dropped. (Readers who have never seen an episode of the old '60s classic *Lost in Space* will not get my Will Robinson reference. That's OK. Just ask your nearest old geek.)

Integer

An integer, as you know, is a whole number. It is declared in Java by using the `int` keyword.

An integer is also signed and two's complement, and it is 32 bits wide, allowing it to hold any value from -2^{31} to $2^{31} - 1$. The default value is zero.

Nothing more to see here. Move along.

Long

As the name suggests, the long gives you more space to hold your big integers. It behaves like an integer in every way, except for two. It can hold any value from -2^{63} to $2^{63} - 1$, and the declaration of a long value requires an `l` or `L` after the number. Convention dictates that you use the capital `L` to avoid confusion with the number one.

Here's an example:

```
long longVar = 12345L;
```

The default value for longs is zero.

Short

There are instances when memory is at a premium. For instance, when you're writing Java code for your HP iPAQ. (Remember, Java is essentially "write once, run anywhere.")

In these situations, you can use the short, which shares all the attributes of an integer but only takes up 16 bits. From this we can deduce its value range to be from -2^{15} to $2^{15} - 1$.

Unlike the long, the short does not require a suffix.

Float

The float data type can hold decimals. As the name suggests, it uses a floating-point precision and can accommodate up to 32 bits. This gives it a value range from $-3.4E38$ to $3.4E38$ and it runs to about 5 or 6 digits of accuracy.

Floats must have an f or an F as a suffix:

```
float f = 12.3456f;
```

Double

The double is similar to the float in many ways except that you obviously declare it with the double keyword. The most important distinction is that it is double (pun intended) the size. The double will hold a stunning 64 bits, which means it can hold values from $-1.7E308$ to $1.7E308$. You *may* append a D or d to the end of the number, but it's optional. Leaving it out will make the assumption of a double.

Although currency calculations would rarely use the full size of a double, it is common practice to use doubles for currency calculations. Large scientific or engineering calculations make good use of the double data type.

Char

The char is the only *unsigned* primitive data type (apart from boolean).

■**Note** Heads up! In C a char is a mere 8 bits wide (255 characters). In Java it is 16 bits wide, allowing for a much greater range of characters. It conforms to Unicode and not to ASCII. (Don't panic, the Unicode and ASCII character sets are identical for the first 255 characters.) This enables us to use Japanese, Chinese, Sanskrit, and many other character sets (for more info, see http://www.unicode.org/charts/).

The char in Java is defined within single quotes. For example,

```
char a = 'A';
```

You can also embed escape sequences within a character definition. Table 3-1 shows a summary of those.

Table 3-1. *Common Escape Sequences*

\n	Linefeed	\r	Carriage return
\f	Form feed	\\	Backslash
\t	Tab	\"	Double quote
\b	Backspace	\'	Single quote

Data Types Summary

That's the lot. Take a moment (get a coffee) and look over what we've learned about primitive data types. Table 3-2 lists them again for your convenience.

Table 3-2. *Summary of Data Types*

Data Type	Size
boolean	true or false
byte	8 bits
short	16 bits
int	32 bits
long	64 bits
float	32 bits
double	64 bits
char	16 bits (unsigned)

In the next lesson we'll cover some commenting standards in Java and have a quick look at the Javadoc utility, which is provided free with the SDK. We'll also have a look at naming conventions and standards.

■ ■ ■

Comments

In this and the next lesson, I'm going to talk about commenting in Java, and then naming conventions and standards. I'm not only going to cover the Sun conventions but also the ones I use to make a program easier to read. This is also known as *good programming style*.

Comments in Java are just like comments in any other language, including ABAP. The one important distinction is that comments can work with the Javadoc utility. This is an extremely powerful tool that will scan your Java program for certain comments, method names, and the like, and produce very nice documentation from it.

Contemporary wisdom dictates that all programs should be fully documented, as this is where you will find developers looking for clues about the program's functionality. Document your programs as much as possible. I do not hold with the notion that because comments may not accurately describe the code, developers can leave them out. All developers benefit from reading commented—even partially commented—programs.

Let's have a look at the three different types of commenting in Java:

- Block comments

- Line comments

- Javadoc comments

Block Comments

Java provides a way of commenting out an entire block of code, as shown here:

```
/* This is a block comment in Java. You may not "nest" block comments in Java.
You can only have one start and one end comment. */
```

Notice the use of /* to start the comment and */ to end the comment.

You can use this form of commenting for a single line, but Java also provides for this with line comments.

Line Comments

Line comments allow you to comment a line, or part of a line. This is very similar to the double quote symbol used in ABAP. Here's an example:

```
int myVariable = 0; // Initialize myVariable to zero.
// Now initialize the other variable.
float myFloat = 3.45f;
```

The two different methods are shown in the preceding example. The double slash // can start at the beginning of a line or halfway through a line, telling the compiler that anything after it is to be ignored.

Javadoc Comments

Javadoc is an incredibly useful utility that actually builds documentation for you! It reads your program comments and method comments and builds a standard form of documentation that every Java programmer can read. Please find the time to research this utility and even to build some skeleton code to see how it works. You can learn all about Javadoc at http://java.sun.com/j2se/javadoc/index.jsp.

Javadoc comments start with /** and end with */. You can also now use tags within your Javadoc comment block, as in this example:

```
/**
Start of comment block.
@author Alistair Rooney
@version 1.1

*/
```

The standard tags are listed at the URL mentioned previously.

Note In Java 5 the tag functionality has been extended. We'll look at this more in Lesson 25, which discusses Enterprise JavaBeans.

LESSON 5

■■■

Naming Standards and Conventions

When talking about naming standards in Java, there are two distinct topics to discuss. The first is the *legality* of the name—will the compiler allow the name—and the second is *popular convention*. The latter will not give you a compiler problem, but it will earn you a sharp smack upside the head from your team leader or fellow developers. I'll let you decide which is worse!

Legal and Illegal Names

As you write your code, you will need to name variables, methods, and labels. Collectively we call the names for these things *identifiers*.

You can start an identifier with any letter, an underscore, or a dollar sign. The identifier can then have any combination of letters or numbers. It can also contain certain special characters, like the underscore. Table 5-1 shows several legal and illegal identifiers—see if you can work out why the names are legal or not.

Table 5-1. *Legal and Illegal Identifiers*

Legal	Illegal
MYVARIABLE	%myVariable
myVariable	My-Variable
my_Variable	9988variable
MyVariable9988	5variable
$myVariable	THE-FIRST-METHOD

While we're on the subject of variable names, let's look at the Java syntax for declaring a variable. In ABAP we would do it as follows:

```
DATA MYVARIABLE TYPE I
```

In Java we would *declare* the variable like this:

```
int myVariable;
```

We can also *initialize* the variable at the same time like so:

```
int myVariable = 76;
```

(In ABAP, we would add the VALUE addition.)

To use the Java equivalent of the chain command in ABAP (DATA:), we can simply use a comma to separate the different variables, *but they must be of the same type*:

```
int myInt1, myInt2, myInt3;
```

This method of defining variables is, however, frowned upon by most developers.

Java Conventions

There are many good sites on the Internet that discuss Java style, and more than one book has been written on this subject alone! I'll just cover the basics of naming conventions here:

- All identifiers should start with a lowercase letter.

- Class names should start with an uppercase letter.

- If there are two words in the name, the second word should always start with an uppercase letter (for example, myGreatVariableName).

- Names should always be meaningful. Do not call your identifiers $a or $b!

- Constants should be *all uppercase* like PI or MYCONSTANT.

Constants are defined using the final keyword. Here's a quick example:

```
final double PI = 3.14159;
```

Remember that a constant cannot be changed in any way. Attempting to do so will throw a compiler error. Constants are also usually prefixed with the static keyword, but this is something we will cover later.

There are other naming suggestions, like prefixing a working variable with an underscore, but these conventions are largely personal preference. For more information about Java coding conventions, look up *Elements of Java Style* by Allan Vermeulen et al., (ISBN: 0-521-77768-2) or take a look at the JavaRanch "Java Programming Style Guide" at http://www.javaranch.com/style.jsp or at Sun's code conventions at http://java.sun.com/docs/codeconv/html/CodeConvTOC.doc.html.

In the next lesson, we will look at the operators that are provided with Java, and at something new to Abapers called *block scope*.

■ ■ ■

The Java Operators

Java operators can be broken down into several different groups:

- Arithmetic operators

- Relational operators

- Increment operators

- Logical operators

We'll look at each of these types in this lesson, along with the concept of block scope.

Arithmetic Operators

The most important thing to remember about arithmetic operators is their *order of precedence*. Let me give you an example:

```
2 + 3 * 5 + 4 = ?
```

If you answered 21, you are correct. If you said 54, you made the mistake of adding the numbers *before* multiplying them. At school we learned about BODMAS, which stands for Brackets, Of, Division, Multiplication, Addition, and Subtraction. Notice how adding and subtracting are the last things you do?

Remember Alistair's golden rule and you'll be OK: *If in doubt, use brackets!* So the previous equation would be better expressed like this:

```
2 + (3 * 5) + 4 = 21
```

These are the math operators in Java:

+	Add
-	Subtract
*	Multiply
/	Divide
%	Modulus

Be careful with the minus sign! It can also be used to denote a negative number. It is a unary operator (meaning it has only one operand).

Relational Operators

Relational operators are usually used when testing the relationship between two variables. There are two big points to remember about relational operators:

- The result of these operations will always return a `true` or `false` boolean value.

- The equals operator is the double equals sign (==) *not* just a single one (=) as in ABAP.

You should be familiar with just about all of the relational operators already:

<	Less than
>	Greater than
==	Equal to
!=	Not equal to
<=	Less than or equal to
>=	Greater than or equal to

Here's a code example:

```java
if (appleCount >= bananaCount)
{
    banana.eat();
}
```

We'll discuss these operators in more detail when we get to the topic of control flow in Lesson 8. Let's move on shall we?

Increment Operators

These are what I call "shorthand" operators:

- The code x = x+1 can be shortened to x++.

- The code y = y-1 can be shortened to y--.

■**Caution** Here's a programmers' joke (but it's not really that funny): Java is the result of the operation C++, since C is only incremented after the operation.

The code for a loop (which we'll cover in Lesson 8) could be like this:

```java
while(x<10)
{
    x++;
    System.out.println("The value of x is  "+x);
}
```

The loop will continue until x equals 10. Notice how x increments each time, as shown in the following output:

```
The value of x is 0
The value of x is 1
The value of x is 2
The value of x is 3
The value of x is 4
The value of x is 5
The value of x is 6
The value of x is 7
The value of x is 8
The value of x is 9
```

Get it?

Now that you have, I'll confuse the issue further. ++x has a slightly different meaning than x++. When the plusses come before the variable name, this tells the interpreter to increment the variable *before* using it.

This means that if we had said x = 3 * j++ and j = 5, then x would equal 15. However if we had said x = 3* ++j, then x would be 18. In other words, in this last case j would already have been incremented to 6 before it was used.

Don't forget this:

- ++h will increment h *before* use.

- h++ will increment h *after* use.

Now look at the joke again! It's still not funny. Let's move on to the next set of operators.

Logical Operators

There are three logical operators. As ABAP programmers you will know these as AND, OR, and NOT. In Java these are the && operator, the || operator, and the ! operator. The first two are the same as in ABAP, but the third has a slightly different meaning. It can negate any Boolean expression, and in doing so, it can be very handy. Commonly these operators are used in if and while statements.

Here's an example:

```
while(x!=10)
{
    x++;
    System.out.println("The value of x is  "+x);
}
```

And here's another:

```
if((a==7)&&(x!=10))
{
    do something . . .
}
```

The first example resolves to "while x is NOT equal to 10." The second one says "if a equals 7 AND x is not equal to 10."

As an ABAP programmer, you should be comfortable with nesting Boolean expressions, so I won't bore you with explanations of these basic principles. However the next section will introduce a new concept: bit manipulation.

Bitwise Operators

There are 8 bits in a byte, and the number 15, for example, is represented as 1111 in binary. Table 6-1 shows it diagrammatically. The sign in our example is positive. If the sign was negative, the leftmost bit would be a 1.

Table 6-1. *Eight Bits Showing the Value 15*

Bit 7	Bit 6	Bit 5	Bit 4	Bit 3	Bit 2	Bit 1	Bit 0
0	0	0	0	1	1	1	1

■Note Negative figures are held in *two's complement* on any computer. Explaining two's complement is not for this course, but feel free to research this if you have the time.

We've digressed a little here. Let's return to our logical operators:

&	ANDs two binary numbers (typically used for masking)
|	ORs two binary numbers (typically used to set bits)
^	XORs a binary number
~	Converts a binary to one's complement
>>	Shifts bits right
<<	Shift bits left
>>>	Shift bits right (logical)

If we were to AND our example value of 15 with 5, we could express this in Java as follows:

```
byte a = (byte) 0x0e;    // 15 in hex
byte b = (byte) 0x05;    // 5 in hex
byte c = (byte)a&b;      // the two are ANDed resulting in 5
```

Table 6-2 shows this diagrammatically. Remember your Boolean logic? *Both* bits must be 1 before the result can be 1. So we have effectively *masked* bits 1 and 3.

Table 6-2. *ANDing 15 and 5*

Bit 7	Bit 6	Bit 5	Bit 4	Bit 3	Bit 2	Bit 1	Bit 0
0	0	0	0	1	1	1	1
0	0	0	0	0	1	0	1
0	0	0	0	0	1	0	1

If we were to OR the same values, we would have the following:

```
byte a = (byte) 0x0e;    // 15 in hex
byte b = (byte) 0x05;    // 5 in hex
byte c = (byte)a|b;      // the 2 are ANDed resulting in 15
```

Table 6-3 shows the diagram. Again Boolean logic dictates that *either* bit can be 1 for the result to be 1. We have *set* bits 1 and 3 in this example.

Table 6-3. *ORing 15 and 5*

Bit 7	Bit 6	Bit 5	Bit 4	Bit 3	Bit 2	Bit 1	Bit 0
0	0	0	0	1	1	1	1
0	0	0	0	0	1	0	1
0	0	0	0	1	1	1	1

To XOR the bits, we use the caret sign (^). This is very useful when working at a bit level, but rarely used in workaday Java. XOR demands that either of the bits may be 1, but not both, to achieve a result of 1.

Shifting operations can also be extremely useful. Let's examine them.

The first is the shift right (>>). We'll use our value of 15 again and shift the bits two to the right:

```
byte a = (byte) 0x0e;    // 15 in hex
byte c = (byte)(a>>2);   // Shifted 2 to the right giving 3
```

Once again, Table 6-4 shows the diagram version.

Table 6-4. *Shifting Bits Two to the Right*

Bit 7	Bit 6	Bit 5	Bit 4	Bit 3	Bit 2	Bit 1	Bit 0
0	0	0	0	1	1	1	1
0	0	0	0	0	0	1	1

You have to be careful with negative numbers, though. Bit 7 is the "sign" bit. For negative numbers, bit 7 would be a 1, and each shift would move a 1 into the leftmost position. The example shown in Table 6-5 demonstrates this. (Remember that negative numbers are held as two's complement in Java. The example in Table 6-5 is not –15.)

Table 6-5. *Shifting Bits Two to the Right in a Negative Number*

Bit 7	Bit 6	Bit 5	Bit 4	Bit 3	Bit 2	Bit 1	Bit 0
1	0	0	0	1	1	1	1
1	1	1	0	0	0	1	1

To *force* the zero to be fed in on the left, regardless of the sign bit, we use the >>> operator. Shifting left is easier, as the bits from the right are always filled with zeroes:

```
byte a = (byte) 0x0e;      // 15 in hex
byte c = (byte)(a<<2);     // Shifted 2 to the left, giving 60
```

Table 6-6 shows this diagrammatically.

Table 6-6. *Shifting Bits Two to the Left*

Bit 7	Bit 6	Bit 5	Bit 4	Bit 3	Bit 2	Bit 1	Bit 0
0	0	0	0	1	1	1	1
0	0	1	1	1	1	0	0

That's all there is for operators!

Block Scope

Conceptually, block scope is a very simple topic. There are just a few basic rules to be followed. First, though, a definition: A *block* is any section of code contained in curly brackets {}. Now for the rules.

Rule number 1: If a variable is defined inside a block, it is not visible to any code outside of that block.

In Java, the following is correctly expressed:

```
{
    int x = 5;
    int y = x + 5;
    System.out.println("x = "+x+" and y = "+y);
}
```

However, the following would produce an error, since the variables are *out of scope*:

```
{
    int x = 5;
    int y = x + 5;
}
System.out.println("x = "+x+" and y = "+y);
```

Rule number 2: If a variable is defined outside a block, it is visible to any code inside that block.

The following Java example would work just fine:

```
int x = 5;
int y = x + 5;
{
    System.out.println("x = "+x+" and y = "+y);
}
```

Easy enough isn't it? In the next lesson we're going to explore the wonders of strings!

Strings with Java

Dealing with text in some way, shape, or form is fundamental to any programming language. Strings can be dealt with using three classes (String, StringBuffer, and StringTokenizer), which you need to get familiar with through your API documentation.

Note I'm not going to cover the Character class here. This is something you can easily research on your own. The Character class is different from the char primitive data type, and it is one example of a *wrapper* class.

THE JAVA API DOCUMENTATION

One of the nicest things about Java is that you can easily see the classes you have available, and the methods you can use in these classes. Simply download and unzip the documentation for your JDK release. The HTML file you need to look at is index.htm in the API directory.

The documentation is in HTML format, and it has a list of all the classes down the left side, and the class details, including the methods, on the right side (see Figure 7-1). Get familiar with this! You'll be using it a lot.

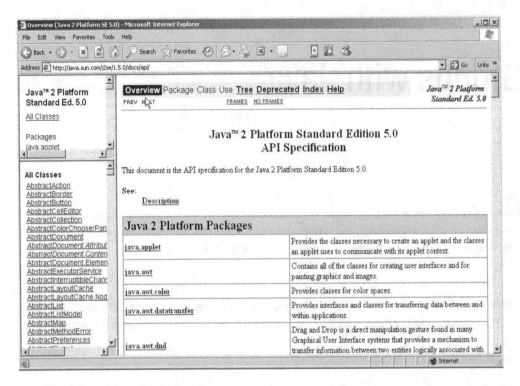

Figure 7-1. *The Java API documentation*

This is the first time we have encountered a *class* that will do our dirty work for us—other languages like ABAP and C use strings as data types. The bonus with Java is that we can use some very powerful methods to work with strings.

Now here's a catch. *Strings are immutable* in Java. This means that you cannot change a String. Before you throw your hands up in horror, though, let me explain a little. I've had students who say to me, "You lied to me—this works fine," and they show me the following code:

```
String myString = "Howdy Podner";
myString = "Hey y'all";
```

After they have finished swearing at me, I tell them that they have not *changed* the string myString; they have *replaced* it entirely, which is a very different thing.

Declaring a String

Formally a String declaration should look like this:

```
String myString = new String("Howdy");
```

This is called *instantiation* in Java. More on this in later lessons.

However, and this is a rather big however, we can declare a String in a shorthand way in Java. We do not have this privilege with other classes in Java (except for one or two, but I'm not telling).

The shorthand declaration is the one we've seen already:

```
String myString = "Howdy Podner";
```

Concatenating Strings

Joining or concatenating strings in Java is very easy. Although we cannot overload operators in Java, Sun has done one for us. The plus (+) sign is used to concatenate two Strings, a char and a String, and just about any other primitive data type.

Let's see an example:

```
String helloString = "Hello";
String worldString = " World";
System.out.println(helloString + worldString);
```

And here's another:

```
String myName = "Alistair";
System.out.println(myName+" is "+21);
```

Which will print out this:

```
Alistair is 21.
```

Using the String Methods

There are over 50 methods in the String class. Obviously, it would be a little silly to cover all of them. I'm going to cover a few basics, and your job is to research the others in the API documentation. I'll introduce each with some code fragments.

The charAt Method

```
String myString = "Welcome";
char firstChar = myString.charAt(3);
```

As you may have guessed, the charAt method returns a character. I have asked it to return the character at position 3, which will be c.

Warning The charAt method requires an integer, and this integer is the *index* of the string. A string's index always starts at 0.

Since this is the first time we have seen a class call, let's direct our attention to the dot operator (the period in `myString.charAt(3)`). This is very similar to the use of `=>` in ABAP. We have the object (reference) `myString`, and we know we want to use the `charAt` method. So we join the two using a dot. For example, `Object.method()`. Don't forget the parentheses.

The substring Method

```
String catMat = "The Cat sat on the Mat";
String catString = catMat.substring(4,7);
```

The catch with the `substring` method is that the start index is normal but the end index requires that you add 1. So to return the string "Cat", we start at 4 and end at 6 + 1, or 7.

As with `charAt`, there is more than one variant of this method, depending on the parameters you want to use.

The equals Method

```
String first = "First String";
String second = "Next one";

if (first.equals(second))
{
    System.out.println("they are equal!");
}
```

This example, using `equals`, compares the values of the two strings.

Hold on. Hold on. Why can't I just use `first == second`? Well I'm glad you asked! The answer is that if you use `==`, you are not actually comparing "First String" and "Next one", you are in fact comparing two object references, which will probably not be equal even if the String *values* are.

So if you want to compare any two object instances using their object references, you should not use the `==` method, you must use the `equals` method. A reference—in case you have not dealt with ABAP objects—is a variable that contains a pointer to an object held in memory, and usually it's just an address.

The length Method

The `length` method is very useful for (surprise!) determining the length of a String.

```
String longOne = "This String is longer than the others";
If (longOne.length() > 20)
{
    do some code here . . .
}
```

You may want to use the `length` method in a loop, but be aware that method calls within loops have a performance overhead. It is better to extract the length outside of the loop.

That's all on String methods. I strongly recommend you read through the API's to see what other methods you have available to you.

Using the StringBuffer Class

The one drawback to using Strings is that they are *immutable*—they cannot be altered *in situ*. The solution to this problem (on the rare occasions it becomes a problem) is to use the StringBuffer class instead of a String or as well as a String. When using StringBuffer, you are free to change the string.

▩**Tip** The StringBuffer is less "expensive" than the String from a performance perspective, and should be used if performance is an issue.

The first thing I need to mention is that if there is a String method to do something, there is probably a StringBuffer method as well. A good example of this is the charAt method.

The following sections concentrate on the methods that are peculiar to the StringBuffer class. Once again, I will be looking at a small selection of the available methods, and I encourage you to read through the APIs.

The append Method

The StringBuffer class must be fully instantiated:

```
StringBuffer sb = new StringBuffer("my jolly string");
sb = sb.append('s');
```

In the preceding example, the character s will be appended to the end of the string, and the instance sb will now contain the string "my jolly strings".

Bear in mind that you can append floats, doubles, integers, and other data types. Have a quick peep at the append methods in the APIs.

Of course Java gives you the ability to insert a data type at a specified position instead of at the end. To do this, you use the insert method.

The insert Method

Continuing the previous example, and assuming the instance sb has been constructed, we could say this:

```
sb = sb.insert(1, 'e');
```

The first parameter is the offset (from 0), and it must be an integer; the second parameter is the character (in this case) that I want to insert. The end result of this operation will have sb containing the string "mey jolly strings".

The other methods in StringBuffer are pretty much self-explanatory. The reverse method does just that—it reverses a String like "abcdefg" and changes the buffer to "gfedcba".

The toString method is handy, but since the String class takes a StringBuffer as an argument in the constructer, we could just say this:

```
String newString = sb.toString();
```

Using the StringTokenizer Class

I don't want to spend longer than a few minutes on this class. It is useful and bears mentioning, but it is something you can look at in more detail on your own.

StringTokenizer will allow the program to run in a loop, examining the contents of a string and breaking it up into separate strings based on the *delimiter* that was specified. This is great for *parsing* XML files and the like (there's more on XML in Lesson 24). You must loop through your string and identify each substring between the delimiters (looping will be covered in Lesson 8).

Here's a quick example:

```
String textExample = "#First String#Second String#Third one";

StringTokenizer st = new StringTokenizer(textExample,"#");

while (st.hasMoreTokens())
{
    String theToken = st.nextToken();
    System.out.println(theToken);
}
```

Note the use of the hasMoreTokens method to check whether we have any left, and the nextToken method to return the next token (strangely enough!) in the String. The preceding example will return the following:

```
First String
Second String
Third one
```

That's all for this lesson! In the next one we'll talk about control flow.

LESSON 8

■■■

Control Flow

A program that hurtles through code in a linear fashion is not terribly exciting. Imagine trying to play a game of chess where you knew all the moves in advance.

I'll say one thing, it's very nice to debug!

Using the if Statement

As you know from ABAP, there are plenty of times where you want to condition your code. In ABAP we use the IF, ELSE, ELSEIF, and ENDIF keywords to introduce decision paths into our code. In Java it's very similar, except that we make use of braces to mark the beginning and end of our code blocks.

Having said that, it is perfectly *legal* to leave the braces off when you have only one line in your if or else statement. Here's an example:

```
if (b==5)
    c = 73;
else
    c = 0;
```

It is *not*, however, professional to do this, as it can easily lead to misinterpretations. You should always use braces with if and else statements, like this:

```
if (b==5)
{
    c = 73;
}
else
{
    c = 0;
}
```

if statements in Java need to be followed by parentheses, and the expression between the parentheses must resolve back to a boolean value. If not, the compiler will tell you when you try to compile the Java program. You should be used to doing this in ABAP, but let's take a quick look at this now!

In ABAP, the expression could be written like this:

```
IF myNewVariable eq wa_newvariable
```

In Java we would write it as follows:

```
if (myNewVariable == wa_newvariable)
```

Notice that in the Java example, the entire condition test is wrapped in parentheses. This ensures that everything between the parentheses can easily be resolved back to a single boolean value—either true or false.

■**Warning** Notice the double equals sign (==) in Java! A single equals in Java is always an assignment, whereas the double equals is the comparison operator.

You are free to do complex comparisons in Java, provided you use the && (and) and the || (or) operators correctly and encase the whole expression in parentheses. Here's an example:

```
if ((a<PI)&&(a>78)||(d==17))
{
. . . code . . .
}
```

Nesting is also available in Java. Remember to indent your code to make it more readable, like this example:

```
if (a<PI)
{
    if (a==73)
    {
        . . . code here . . .
    }
}
```

There can be multiple levels of nesting, but remember that this can obfuscate your logic, so beware. If you find yourself going down more than five levels, have a long hard look at your program design. One way to get around too many nested if statements is to use the switch statement, discussed later in this lesson.

There is a shortcut operator in Java for writing an if statement in one line. It is the ? operator.

Using the ? and : Operators

You can replace the traditional if operator with the ? operator for true values and the : operator for false values.

Here's an example using the if operator:

```
if (b==5)
    c = 73;
else
    c = 0;
```

The preceding statement can be written like this:

```
c = (b==5)?73:0;
```

In other words, if b equals 5, the c is set to the value after the ? (73), else the value would be set to whatever follows the : (0).

Pretty smooth! This is nice for embedding within other code, like this:

```
System.out.println("The answer is "+(b==5)?73:0);
```

So far so good. All of this should be second nature to anyone who has programmed before. Now on to the switch statement.

Using the switch Statement

The switch statement is a little disappointing in Java. In ABAP and in other languages, we have powerful case statements that can check each level individually. In Java, though, each case within the switch statement must be terminated with a break statement.

■**Note** The switch statement can only test an int, byte, short, or char.

Let's have a look at the switch statement in action:

```
int option = x;
switch(option)
{
    case 1:
        System.out.println("You selected 1");
        break;
    case 2:
        System.out.println("You selected 2");
        break;
    case 3:
        System.out.println("You selected 3");
        break;
    default:
        System.out.println("You selected something else");
        break;
}
```

Notice the default statement. This bears some resemblance to the WHEN OTHERS statement in ABAP. In other words, it acts as a catchall for anything that has not been processed by the preceding case statements. It is always good practice to include one default statement to ensure your logic does not contain any holes.

Not very difficult is it? But it is a little limited, as I mentioned.

Looping

In most programming languages we have the ability to iterate around a segment of code. This is called *looping* (but you knew that already). In ABAP, we have a number of options open to us, some of which are peculiar to the language. For example, the LOOP AT keyword is probably the most common iteration in ABAP, and yet it does not exist outside of ABAP. This is mostly because of the unique concept of internal tables.

In any case, there are two distinct ways of looping: test-before loops and test-after loops.

In ABAP we have DO, WHILE, and even CHECK. DO can test at the beginning and anywhere between the start and end of the loop, using the EXIT keyword to leave. WHILE will only test at the beginning.

We have three types of loops available to us in Java: while, for, and do.

The while Loop

The equivalent of the ABAP WHILE loop is the—wait for it—Java while loop. Yup, it is that easy. The syntax is almost identical. We say while (expression), and we use our curly braces to denote our loop scope.

As with all these statements in Java, we are allowed to forego the use of curly braces if we have only one line in our loop. However, as was mentioned earlier, you should always use the braces (curly brackets) regardless of the number of lines.

INTERNAL TABLES AND THE JAVA CONNECTOR (JCO) FROM SAP

SAP has provided us with a very useful tool to connect to SAP systems from within Java: the Java Connector (JCo). How to use JCo is discussed in Lesson 20, but one interesting thing is that it has the ability to duplicate a SAP data dictionary type (like a structure) within the Java realm. Using this we can build internal tables using JCO.Table *within our Java program!* They could have used arrays, but this little trick is very cool, and for this SAP wins the coveted "cool API of the week" award.

Let's have a look at a trivial code fragment to demonstrate the while loop:

```
public void myLoopMethod(int noOfTimes)
{
    int n = 0;
    // Loop while n is less than noOfTimes
    while (n<noOfTimes)
    {
        n++;
        System.out.println("n is now "+n);
        System.out.println("n is now " + n++);
    }
}
```

We can see that this method (myLoopMethod) takes an integer as a parameter. The while loop repeats the number of times specified in the integer. It keeps a count using the variable n, and it prints out the result on each iteration.

Notice how this is a very good example of testing at the beginning of a loop. Easy so far!

Warning Beware putting a semicolon at the end of the while line. This will result in a functionless loop!

The for Loop

In ABAP we have some very handy things called internal tables. To loop through the internal table, you just use LOOP AT. You know that it will step through the internal table incrementing by 1 each time.

In Java we have to specify our starting position in the structure (an array, for example) and how big our increment steps should be. To do all of this, we use the following syntax:

```
for(int i=0; i<10; i++)
{

//Do some code

}
```

The for statement can be broken down into three substatements that are separated by semicolons (*not* commas):

- The first initializes the variable or variables you wish to use in your loop. You can also declare your variable here, which is pretty neat. In the preceding example, you can see that I've done just that.

- The second section works best if you say "while" to yourself before reading it. You've guessed it—this is the condition section, and it must resolve back to a single boolean value. So in our example the loop will continue "while" i is less than 10.

- The third section increments or decrements one or more variables. Obviously, in the preceding example, I wanted to increment by 2 at a time. You can, of course, do the increment manually. Here's a quick example:

```
for(int i=0; i<10; i=i+2)
{

//Do some code

}
```

It is legal to have empty sections or substatements. In fact, some people recommend the following for triggering an endless loop (I prefer while(true)):

```
for(;;);
```

That's the short story of for loops. When we examine arrays in Lesson 10, I will spend a little more time on them.

The do Loop

I can tell you're not "loopy" enough yet, so I'll carry on with the next loop. This is where a test is done at the end of the loop, as opposed to the beginning. All good programming languages should have one of these loops, as it saves you from slipping into unstructured code (like using the ABAP EXIT statement!). I disagree strongly with some Java authors who recommend not using it. I find it very useful.

The way that we do this in Java is by using the do . . . while loop. Let's have a look at this in a code snippet:

```
do
{

System.out.println("The value of x is "+x++);

} while(x<10);
```

Don't get confused by the x++. Remember that this will just increment the variable after it has been printed.

Note The most important point about this form of loop is that it will be run *at least* once.

As you can see, loops are quite straightforward. You can, of course, nest any loop within any other loop.

Next we will have a quick look at jump statements.

■■■

Jump Statements

There is a way in Java to leave a loop prematurely, just as you can do with the ABAP EXIT or CONTINUE statements. In fact, there are several ways to do this. They are collectively called the *jump* statements.

Tip Try *not* to use jump statements. They promote exceptionally unstructured code, which at its worst will turn into the dreaded "spaghetti code." There is almost *always* a way to design your code so that you don't have to use them.

The break Statement

The first of the jump statements is one that you cannot avoid if you choose to use the switch statement. This is break.

The break statement can be used in any loop—it is not restricted to the switch statement. If it is encountered in a normal while loop, it will leave processing of the loop at that point and continue with the next statement outside of the loop. This will happen regardless of the condition in the loop.

In the following example, we leave the loop whenever the variable equals 7. (Yes, it's a silly example, because we'll never reach 8 or 9, but it's just an illustration.)

```
for(int i=0; i<10; i++)
{

if (i=7)
    break;

}
```

The continue Statement

The next keyword is a little less evil. This is the `continue` statement. With this you can move on to the next iteration of the loop, and any unprocessed lines in that iteration will be ignored. In other words, the control will leave the loop at the point of the `continue` and will start at the top of the loop on the next cycle.

Try to avoid using this one in Java, but you can still use it in ABAP if you like!

The return Statement

Unlike the others, the `return` statement is very useful. It can be used in a method to return control to the calling method, and it can pass one parameter.

Here's a wee example:

```
public double calcArea(double radius)
{
    area = Math.PI*radius*radius;
    return area;
}
```

You can have more than one `return` statement in a method, but they are usually controlled by a condition—you would only execute one at a time.

You may not have a `return` that returns nothing if you have specified that there is a return type on the method signature. That might sound a bit confusing, so I'll explain. In a method you may explicitly specify that there is no return parameter, and to do this we use the keyword void. When we use void, we are not allowed to pass back any variable. In such a case, the `return` statement could be on its own, or you can choose to omit it. In the following example, it's used on its own:

```
public void setArea(double area)
{
    this.area = area;
    return; // Optional in this case
}
```

In the `calcArea` method above we have *explicitly* specified that we will return a double, so when we use the `return` statement we need to specify a double type of variable. (More on this in Lesson 11 where we'll cover classes and objects.)

That's all for this lesson. Tune in next time when we will start to explore the wonderful world of arrays and collections!

LESSON 10

■ ■ ■

Arrays and Collections in Java

If you're an ABAP programmer and you haven't coded in other languages, you may not have come across *Arrays*. However, you've been using them all along (in a way) without being aware of it.

In ABAP we have internal tables, which are basically *collections*. There are three basic types of internal tables in ABAP: standard, sorted, and hashed. How you use each of these depends on the access method you choose.

Arrays (and other collections) in Java are more "manual" than in ABAP. You must code the loop yourself—sadly you can't just say LOOP AT and have your table be read to the end. Cast your mind back to the for loop we covered in the last lesson—this is the primary mechanism we will use for reading an Array.

There are many collections in Java. In this section I will cover Arrays and touch on Vectors.

I strongly urge you to review the Java API documentation at this point, as a full understanding of the structure of these classes is extremely useful.

Using Arrays

In case you're still lost and have no idea what I am talking about, I'll provide some basic examples. (If you're comfortable with the concept of Arrays, you can skip this section, but look at the Java syntax.)

There are many Array analogies, but the one I'm most comfortable with when explaining single-dimension arrays is the pigeonhole system. In a hotel, for example, there are a number of pigeonhole slots where the staff can put any number of items for guests to collect at their leisure. Let's say our hotel has only ten rooms:

0	1	2	3	4	5	6	7	8	9

I can put anything I like into those little pigeonholes: a Java primitive data type (an int or a double, for example) or an object (String, for example). I can even put another Array into an Array. So, to extend our analogy slightly, we would be putting another whole row of boxes inside one pigeonhole.

However, an Array may only have *one* type of entry for the entire array. You may not "mix and match" your data types within an Array.

■**Note** In the preceding diagram, you'll notice that I've started counting at *zero*, not at one. In Java we count Arrays from zero. In ABAP the first line of the internal table is `sy-tabix = 1`.

The Array Index

Just like we have `sy-tabix` in ABAP, we have an index for our Java Arrays. The index will point at one pigeonhole or *element* at a time.

If you are familiar with C or C++, you will be aware of the infamous ability of C to read *beyond the end* of an Array without even so much as a murmur from the runtime! Thankfully, we cannot do this in Java without causing a runtime exception to be thrown.

Declaring an Array

If you want to go on and study for your Sun certification, you need to be aware of the three distinct stages for Arrays: declaring, creating, and filling. We can do all three at once, but let's break it down into those different steps.

Declaring an Array is very easy. Let's declare an Array of Strings.

```
String[] myArray ;
```

Notice the square brackets. These tell us that we are declaring an Array of Strings and not just one String. It is important to note that the square brackets can come after the identifier (myArray), if you choose, like this:

```
String myArray[];
```

Just be consistent.

■**Tip** It is conventional to put the brackets after the data type, as in the first example, so don't be too shocked if you attract a rude comment for coding differently.

Creating the Array

We haven't told the compiler much about our Array yet, so let's do that by creating or *instantiating* our Array.

```
myArray = new String[10];
```

Note We will explore the new keyword more fully when we examine objects in Lesson 11.

Before we move on to filling our Array, let's look at how we could combine the first two stages into one line of code. It's easy:

```
String[] myArray  = new String[10];
```

Filling the Array

There are basically two ways to fill an array: the wrong way and the right way.

I'm not a fan of *any* hard-coded content in a program, so I'm very much against hard-coding your array entries, which is the first way of filling arrays. You can declare, create, and fill an array by using this hard-coded method:

```
String[] myArray  = new String{"One", "Two", "Three", "Four", "Five"};
```

As you can see, it's a very effective way to define an array, but since hard-coding should be anathema to professional programmers, I advise against its use.

The correct way to populate an array is with variables, and the most common way to do this is with the for loop we learned about in Lesson 9. Here's an example:

```
String[] myArray  = new String[10];

for (int i=0; i<myArray.length; i++)
{
    myArray[i] = "String number"+i;
}
```

Notice in the preceding example how each array element is referenced by saying myArray[n], where the value of n is the element number we want to reference.

Also, remember that Java arrays start at *zero*. This is why we only want to loop while the variable i is less than the length of the array. This is clearer in a diagram—on the top is the natural number (1 to 10) indicating the position in the Array, and below is the index number for that Array position. When you reach the end of the Array, the index value will be one less than the Array's length.

```
1    2    3    4    5    6    7    8    9    10
-----------------------------------------------
0    1    2    3    4    5    6    7    8    9
```

Note length is a variable of the Array class and not a method, so there are no brackets. More on methods in Lesson 11.

Multidimensional Arrays

In Java we can have multidimensional Arrays. A two-dimensional Array is very similar to an Excel spreadsheet: you can have multiple rows with varying numbers of columns in each. If the number of columns is identical in each row, we have a *rectangular* 2-D Array. If they are not equal, we have what is called a *staggered* Array.

I don't want to go into too much detail on 2-D arrays, but I do want to show you how to declare them:

```
String[] [ ] myArray  = new String[5] [5];
```

This will create a five-by-five rectangular (actually square!) Array. This means that for each element in the primary array, there is another entire array that is five elements long.

That's all I want to say about Arrays for now. Let's move on to other Collections.

The Vector Class

The Java Collections can be seen more clearly in Figure 10-1, which is from Sun.

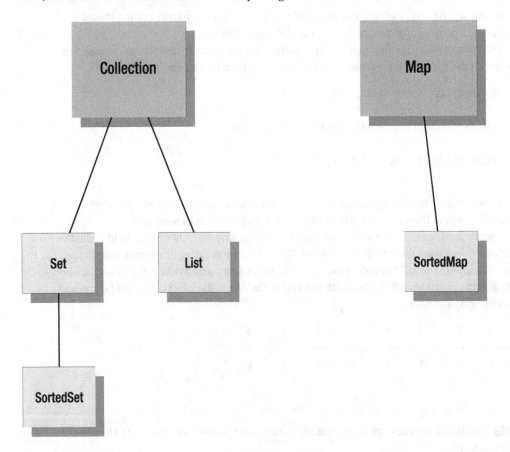

Figure 10-1. *Collections schematic from Sun Microsystems*

The Vector class is a member of the List class (have a look at the APIs in Figure 10-2). As such it behaves very much like an Array. One main difference between a Vector and an Array is that a Vector can grow. Or to put it another way, the Vector will dynamically allocate space. A Vector can also mix its element types, which is pretty useful! However a Vector may only contain objects and not primitive data types. Instead of using Vectors, though, most developers tend to use the ArrayList class, which shares some of the characteristics of the Vector.

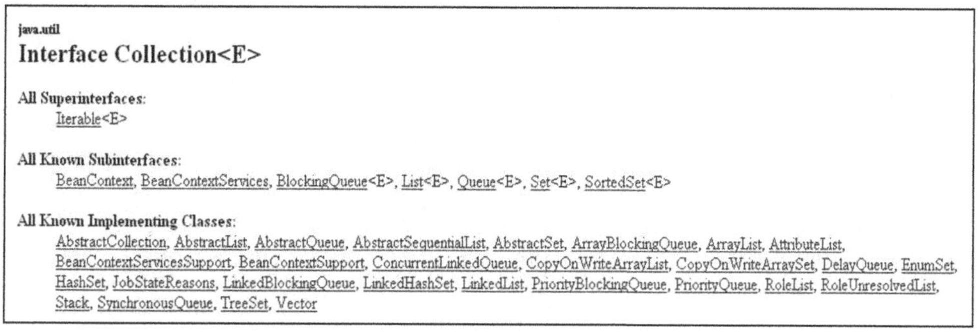

Figure 10-2. *API documentation for the Collection Interface*

Using Vectors

To add an element to a Vector, you use the addElement() method.

To loop through the elements of a Vector, you can set up an Enumerator and use it to check whether the Vector has more elements by using the enum.hasMoreElements() method.

I won't go into detail here, but I encourage you to look at one of the many sites discussing Vectors and other collections on the Internet.

That's it for collections. Next we will look at classes and methods.

■■■

Object Orientation in Java

Ah, objects. Some people take to object orientation (OO) like a duck to water. Most people don't really get it for a while (6 to 18 months). But when they do get it, they become evangelists for OO.

I coded procedural programs for close on 18 years before embarking on this OO journey. Although I learned Java in 1997, I treated it like another C. In 1999, however, a gifted man (Stuart Fripp) introduced me to OO and UML. I liked what I saw and started using it in my projects. It was only in late 2000 that I felt I was designing properly in OO.

I tell you this story so that you will persevere with OO. It is difficult to convert from procedural to object oriented programming, but please don't give up. The benefits are real and very cool.

By the way, does SAP "get" OO? They are certainly on the right path.

The Pillars of OO

These are the four pillars of OO:

- Inheritance

- Encapsulation

- Abstraction

- Polymorphism

It is very difficult to talk about inheritance without discussing polymorphism, so I'll deal with those two together. First, though, I would like to discuss the structure of a Java class.

Java Class Structure

Figure 11-1 shows a simple diagram of a Java class. The outside box is the class container—we define a class in Java using the `class` keyword.

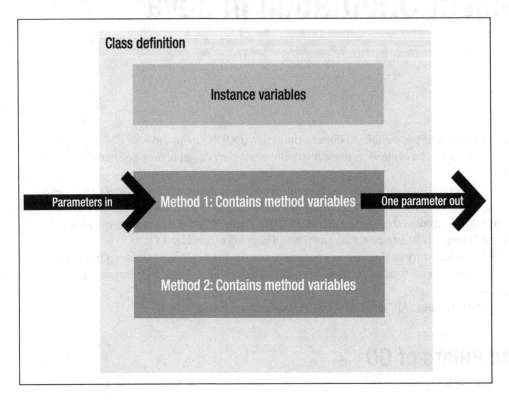

Figure 11-1. *Java class schematic*

Between the class definition and the first method, we can declare our instance variables. These are variables you would like the whole class to see (although it's *not* the same thing, you can think of these as global variables for the class). If you define something in Method 1, it is not visible to Method 2—remember the discussion of block scope in Lesson 6? However, if you define an instance variable, it is available to all methods.

The two big arrows in the figure are both optional. In Java, the absence of a return (or outbound) parameter is shown by using `void` in the method declaration. If we have no inbound parameters, we show this by having empty brackets ( ) in the method declaration.

■**Note** Notice that the outbound arrow carries a single parameter. Only one parameter can be "exported" (to borrow an ABAP term).

I hear you screech with horror! OK, maybe you just raised an eyebrow. Yes, Java will only allow *one* parameter to be returned from a method. But this is good. It will force you to implement methods correctly: A method must do one thing, and one thing only! This will force us to start thinking in an object way.

Inheritance and Polymorphism

One of the great things about an OO programming language is the concept of *inheritance*.

Suppose I have already coded a generic BankAccount class. Why should I code a completely new class for a credit card account, or a savings account, or even a checking account? Wouldn't it be great if I could just *reuse* the standard functionality that I (or some other programmer) had already created in the plain old BankAccount class?

With inheritance, you can. By simply using the extends keyword in Java, we can use all the methods that we are allowed to use. (We'll look at access modifiers later, but it is sufficient to say here that if we want to prevent inheritance, we can do so. For example, try to write a program that extends the String class.)

Let's look at a model to see how inheritance works. This model won't be realistic—there are no databases here, the account balance is somehow magically held by the object, and so on. Bear with me, this is just an example. I'll extend it a bit in the future.

The generic BankAccount class will never be *instantiated* directly. In Lesson 7 we created an instance of the String class like this (or said we could have):

```
String s = new String("Hello");
```

The new keyword means that a new instance of the class has been created, and we have called it s.

Let's briefly take a step back. Think of your class as being the design or specification for an object—the blueprint of a house, for example. A house can be built many times from one set of blueprints, and similarly, many objects can be instantiated from one class.

Cast your mind back to Lesson 2, and you'll recognize Figure 11-2, which represents the BankAccount class. We can see that it holds a private attribute and four public methods. (And you can see that I'm not sticking to strict UML notation here. Please don't report me to the OO police just yet!)

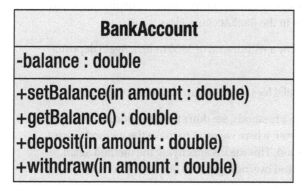

Figure 11-2. *The BankAccount class*

We can now create the classes for the three other types of accounts we want to "inherit from" our BankAccount class: the CreditCard class, the SavingsAccount class, and the Check-Account class. To show inheritance in UML, we draw the classes as we would draw an organizational diagram—take a look at Figure 11-3.

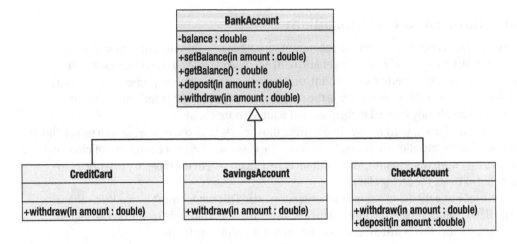

Figure 11-3. *Inheriting from the BankAccount class*

So, let's look at what we're doing here. The three subclasses of the BankAccount class inherit all the methods from the BankAccount class, free of charge. So if you have some superb functionality in your BankAccount class (also known as the *superclass*), you already have it in your subclass just by saying that the subclass extends the superclass.

If we were to look at the class signature of the SavingsAccount class, we would see this:

```
class SavingsAccount extends BankAccount
```

As a result, we do not have to recode any of the methods contained in the BankAccount class. We get them automatically. Now is that cool or what? This is the basic premise of inheritance.

That's great, but what if you need something different in one of the classes?

- Funds cannot be withdrawn from the credit card account. However, depositing funds for the CreditCard class is the same as in the BankAccount class.

- The SavingsAccount class will only allow a withdrawal of $500 or less. Again deposits are standard.

- The CheckAccount class will have special fees for withdrawals and deposits.

Where we just want to use the superclass's methods, we don't need to code a line! Remember, we inherit all of that functionality! However, where we want to make the method more *specialized*, we will have to *override* the method. This means specifying the method again, ignoring the functionality in the superclass, and overriding it with our own. Overriding is the first part of *polymorphism*.

METHOD SIGNATURES: OVERRIDING VS. OVERLOADING

The term "method signature" basically means "the syntax of the method definition." A method can have a return type or nothing at all (void) and the method can accept parameters as well. These attributes make up the method signature.

If you define a method in the subclass with the same name of a method in the superclass, and the method signature differs, you are, in effect, *overloading* the method. If the method signature remains the same, you are *overriding* the method. Obviously the method name remains the same, and remember, it's case-sensitive.

Suppose that there are two types of withdrawals that can be made from our CheckAccount class: the withdrawal amount can be a BigDecimal type or a double. We can cater for this by duplicating our withdrawal method, and just having the method signatures differ. Our double method will have this signature:

```
public void withdrawal(double amount)
```

The BigDecimal method will have this signature:

```
public void withdrawal(BigDecimal amount)
```

This technique is called *overloading*, and the really smart thing about Java is that the correct method to be called is only determined *at run time*. (As an exercise, write a little program to test this feature, called *late binding* in Java.)

Tip Keep in mind that this is just an introduction to Java. I recommend you read Bruce Eckel's *Thinking in Java* for a good explanation of these concepts (http://www.bruceeckel.com).

Encapsulation

Encapsulation is the "hiding" of methods and data. I like to think of a wooden box with several partitions that only has one opening to the outside world (see Figure 11-4). All data must pass through this one hole.

Notice how I've called the area that is directly accessible "public," and the area that is not directly accessible "private." We'll cover these terms again in a moment, but you can see that I can hide my data away in the private area.

So why would I want to hide things from my fellow programmers? Is it because I don't trust them? No, of course not. I'm going to let people who use my class, do so in the way I want them to use it.

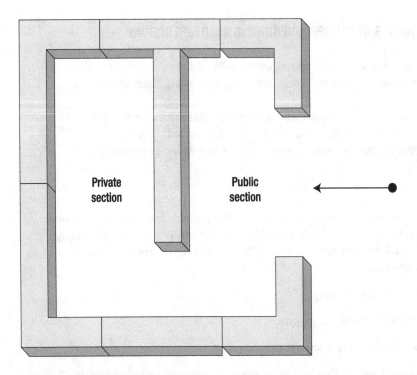

Figure 11-4. *The wooden box analogy*

For example, car manufacturers expect us to use the gas pedal to make the car go faster and the brake to slow it down. The manufacturers don't want us messing with the engine directly to speed up or slow down, so they give us a convenient, standard, and predictable way to interact with it. They encapsulate the engine behind a firewall (the real kind).

We want to do the same thing with our classes. Not through arrogance or malice, but so that people can use them in a stable and predictable manner, which will make the resulting code more robust.

Let's have a look at an example. We need to calculate a mortgage payment, and we are given the principal amount, the number of periods, and the interest rate. Our class will have a few methods: the constructor, a getRepayment method, and a calcLoan method.

If we are good OO programmers, we will make the calcLoan method private. This will prevent inheritance and force the user of the class to use the getRepayment method to return the actual repayment. Let's look at the code to make it clearer.

```java
public class Loans
{
// Our instance variables - notice they are private
private double principal;
private double periods;
private double interest;
private double repayment;
```

```
// This is the Constructor - more about it later
   public Loans(double principal, double periods, double int)
   {
       this.principal = principal;
       this.periods = periods;
       interest = int;
       calcLoan();
   }

// This method calculates the loan - let's not worry how!
   private void calcLoan()
   {
       // code here to do the work! Updates repayment.
   }

// Now we allow the class user to access the repayment amount
   public double getRepayment()
   {
       return repayment;
   }
} // end of class
```

I want to point out several things in this code. The first is that I am "hiding" the class variables. I do not want anyone to mess with these, so I declared my variables private.

So if the variables are hidden, how do I pass the necessary information to the class? I do this by means of a special *once only* method called a *constructor*. The constructor cannot have *any* return type, not even *void*. It must also have *exactly* the same name as the class.

The constructor's primary job is to initialize instance variables, and we call it after the new keyword. Here's what it would look like in the calling program:

```
Loans ln = new Loans(250000.00, 240.00, 5.00);
```

Notice how the constructor of the Loans class is called after the new keyword.

If you understand how block scope works, you will realize that the instance variable principal and the variable principal declared in the method signature of the constructor are *two different variables*! To confuse the issue further, they have exactly the same name. Tricky, hey!

Fortunately we can use a special this keyword, which tells us (and the Java compiler) that we are talking about the *instance variable* and not the variable defined in the method. You can see that since I don't have that problem with interest and int, I do not have to use the this keyword. By the way, we can use the this keyword to denote methods as well. If you want to specify a method from the current class, you could (optionally) use this to make it clear.

The last line in the constructor calls the calcLoan method.

The next method, the calcLoan method, I've declared as private. This effectively means that it can only be used from within its own class. It can't be inherited, and it can't be seen until an instance of this class is created. This is fine with me. It's a complex method, and only my class knows how to use it properly. Encapsulation is great. It maintains the integrity of my class, even when it is used by other classes.

Finally, I still need to get my repayment amount out of this class. For situations like this, we create special methods that are usually prefixed by get or set. Some people call these *getter* and *setter* methods or *accessor* and *mutator* methods. Basically, they allow us to get or set private instance variables.

We only need access to one instance variable, repayment, so we need an accessor method to retrieve it. It is the last method in our code, the getRepayment method. As you can see, it merely returns a double to our calling program. We would code the calling program as follows:

```
double repay = ln.getRepayment();
```

Notice that I used the instance of Loans, ln, that I created earlier. Notice also that, as in ABAP, the names do not have to match, but the types of the variables must match.

I hope I haven't confused you too much with this discussion of encapsulation. Read as much about it as you can, as it really is a cornerstone of Java.

Abstraction

I don't intend spending much time on this topic. Abstraction and encapsulation are opposite sides of the same coin. I may have a very complex television set, but I don't want to know how it works. The buttons (the interface) on the TV, or on the remote, are all I care about. The complexity is hidden (*encapsulated*), and all I see is the simple representation of the object, in other words an *abstraction*.

If you take a UML course, you will learn about conceptualizing the problem domain. In plain English, that means using abstraction to create concepts like a Bank Account. This is the process of abstraction.

Let's move on to such gems as abstract classes and interfaces.

■ ■ ■

More OO in Java—Interfaces and Abstract Classes

In Java there is officially no "multiple inheritance." You may extend one class, and one class only! Having said that, though, we can simulate multiple inheritance in Java by using interfaces. This is *not* what interfaces are for! It is just an interesting side effect.

More on this later. First, let's discuss abstract classes, which are never instantiated, only inherited.

Abstract Classes

Declaring a class `final` will effectively prevent that class from having subclasses. In other words, there is no way you can inherit from a final class (try it with String or Math).

```
final class NoSubs
{
```

The opposite of this is an abstract class. You must have a subclass somewhere for the abstract class to work.

An abstract class should have at least one abstract method (although, for some strange reason, it is not mandatory). A common mistake amongst students of Java is to assume that abstract classes must have abstract methods, but please think about this the other way around: *If you have an abstract method, you must declare the class as abstract!* This means you may have ten methods, but if only one is abstract, then you have an abstract class.

Here is how we declare an abstract class (I've included an abstract method so that you can become familiar with them):

```
abstract class MustHaveSubs
{
    String longName = " ";

    public String getName()
    {
        return longName;
    }

    public abstract void setName(String name);
}
```

Notice how I have an abstract method defined (setName(String name)) and I have a normal accessor (getter) method called getName.

In essence, what I am saying here is that whoever uses or "implements" this class may override the getName method, but they are *forced* to override *and* implement the setName method. This means that the class's designer knows enough to force you to implement the method but not enough to code the functionality for you.

Let's look at a contrived example. I am designing a banking system, and I know enough to say with a certain amount of confidence that all my bank account classes will have at least methods for depositing and withdrawing funds, as shown in Figure 12-1. I'm confident of this, but I'm not sure how all my different classes will implement this. So I make the methods abstract so that my bank account subclasses will bear the responsibility for implementing them.

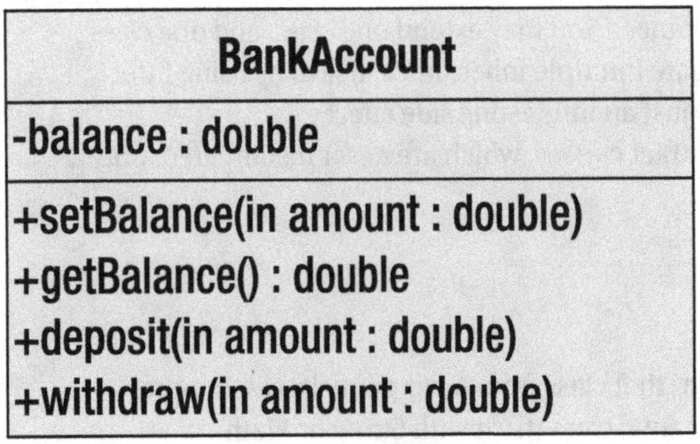

BankAccount
-balance : double
+setBalance(in amount : double) +getBalance() : double +deposit(in amount : double) +withdraw(in amount : double)

Figure 12-1. *The BankAccount class*

■**Tip** Abstract methods are implicitly public, but have pity on the poor maintenance programmer and declare them public anyway.

I may also have methods to get and set the balance (and since I am a good OO programmer, I have made balance private). Even in the early stages of my design, I know how these should be coded. Therefore they are not defined as abstract. However, this does not prevent the implementer from overriding these methods and extending or replacing the code.

■**Note** When a method is overridden, you cannot make it more private than it already is. Also an overridden method cannot throw more exceptions than the method in the superclass. (We'll cover exception handling in Lesson 14.)

If I wanted to make all the methods abstract I could do, but there is a better mechanism for doing this called an *interface*. Think of the abstract class as being a template for a class; an interface is a blueprint so that you can build a template.

Interfaces

When I consider interfaces, I always think of three things a great Java lecturer, Casper Baden-horst, told me:

- An interface is a more abstract class than an abstract class.

- An interface makes a promise, or contract, that the methods will be implemented.

- Using interfaces can allow you to simulate multiple inheritance.

If you remember those three things, you'll be halfway there.

An interface is a template for a class. As with abstract classes, we know what methods should be in the class (because we've done our design properly), but we don't know how they will be implemented. Unlike abstract classes, *all* the methods in an interface must be abstract. They can have no implementation. Common interfaces in Java are Runnable, ActionListener, and WindowListener.

Here's an example of an interface:

```
public interface Shape
{
    float calcArea(double x, double y);
}
```

Notice how we have no curly brackets after the method declaration, and how we don't put the word *abstract* in at all. As I mentioned previously, all methods must be abstract in an interface, so there is little need to declare them abstract.

So how do we use this interface in our class? We implement our interface using the—you guessed it—implements keyword. Here's an example of implementing the Shape interface:

```
public class Square implements Shape
{
    public float calcArea(double x, double y)
    {
        float area = (float)x*y;
        return area;
    }
}
```

Any ideas why I must cast (float) before putting a value into area? You are right! Both the variables x and y are doubles, so casting must take place.

We can also subclass an interface with another interface by just saying extends. Surprisingly we can have more than one superclass for an interface. So we could say that interface A extends B, C, and D. Of course B, C, and D must be interfaces to allow this.

Another interesting aspect of interfaces is that Java will allow you to define variables in your interface, but they will automatically be declared `static` and `final`. This makes sense (to me, at any rate) since these should only be constants.

Tip As I've mentioned before, this is merely an introduction to Java—there is much more to this subject than will fit in this book. Understanding classes and objects is fundamental to becoming a good Java programmer, so *please* explore this subject further.

In the next lesson we will explore nested, inner, and anonymous classes.

■■■

Inner, Nested, and Anonymous Classes

Inner, nested, and anonymous classes are all classes within classes, and there's a debate that takes place around this subject. I'll put the arguments forward for both schools of thought:

- **School of thought one:** Do not use anonymous classes, period. They can get completely out of hand, they obfuscate the code, they are unwieldy, and some software, like Ant, does not deal with them effectively enough.

- **School of thought two:** You can use anonymous classes, but make sure they are short, not complex (have only one method), predictable, and easy to understand.

Unless there are software conflicts, I put myself firmly in the second camp (and according to a recent study, 70 percent of developers feel the same way). Of course, you (or your development manager) can decide for yourself.

Inner Classes

Basically speaking, an *inner* class is simply a class within another class—these are also known as *local* classes. Inner classes have access to the instance members of the outer class.

Note Most Java lecturers will tell you to put inner classes inside a method of the outer class. Although this is a common use of the inner class, it is not a requirement.

Here is a trivial example of an inner class:

```
/*
 * Simple Inner Class example
 */

import java.applet.*;
import java.awt.*;
import java.awt.event.*;
```

```
class JavaBook1 extends Applet
{
    Button press = new Button("Click here!");

    public void init()
    {
        class InnerClassExample implements ActionListener
        {
            public void ActionPerformed(ActionEvent ae)
            {
                System.out.println("The Button was pressed");
            }
        }
        add(press);
        press.addActionListener(new InnerClassExample());
    }

}
```

I know we haven't covered applets in any great detail, but you should be able to see what's going on here. (If you're confused after you read my explanation here, take a look at Lesson 17, on event handling.)

The init method is fired off automatically in an applet. This method contains an inner class, which you can see implements an interface called ActionListener. We'll cover this in Lesson 17, but simply put, this interface will help us deal with a button click.

One button (press) is defined in this program, and the inner class uses one method (ActionPerformed) to do something when the button is pressed—in this example, it just prints out a message that says "The Button was pressed".

Outside of the inner class, the button is added to the applet, and the last line of the init method adds an ActionListener to the button. The ActionListener is an instance of the InnerClassExample class.

The ActionListener could, of course, be implemented in a more elegant way with an anonymous class, but we'll get to that later.

Nested Classes

The main difference between an inner and a nested class is that a nested class can be declared as static. Just remember that static classes can not access nonstatic instance variables or methods from the outer class.

Also it's worth pointing out that nested classes generally do not live in a method of the outer class.

Anonymous Classes

While the inner class and, for that matter, the nested class, enables us to keep our common code local, there is another option: the *anonymous* class. As the name suggests, this is an unnamed class that we want to create an instance of. All of the code for the anonymous class is coded within the method where we need to create an instance of the anonymous class.

If you are going to use an anonymous class, keep in mind the rules:

- Keep it small.

- Keep it simple (only one method).

- Make it easy to understand. Commonly used code is OK here.

Let's look at an example. This is the example we looked at earlier, with the inner class changed to an anonymous class:

```java
/*
 * Simple Anonymous Class example
 */

import java.applet.*;
import java.awt.*;
import java.awt.event.*;

class JavaBook1 extends Applet
{
    Button press = new Button("Click here!");

    public void init()
    {
        add(press);
        press.addActionListener(new  ActionListener()
            {
                public void actionPerformed(ActionEvent ae)
                {
                    System.out.println("The Button was pressed");
                }
            }
        );
    }
}
```

As you can see, the entire `actionPerformed` method goes into the argument for the addActionListener class. Pretty neat, hey! You will see how often we use this method when we discuss event handling in Lesson 17. Notice the new keyword—the instantiation is performed instantly on this class.

Incidentally, when this code is compiled, you have *two* class files: one called `JavaBook1.class` and one called `JavaBook1$1.class` for the anonymous class.

Next we will explore the important topic of errors and exceptions!

LESSON 14

■ ■ ■

Errors and Exceptions

Java has a much more formal approach to exception handling than other languages (like C). In ABAP we tend to rely on dandy system variables like sy-subrc. This is fine, but nothing forces you to deal with potential errors. You are not obliged to check your sy-subrc variable after a SELECT statement, but most people do because it's good programming practice. In Java you are obliged to check for exceptions.

Of course, you will hopefully find most of your potential errors in code when you compile your program or class. The latest generation of IDEs, like Eclipse (http://www.eclipse.org) and Netbeans (http://java.sun.com) will even highlight your errors as you code, which is rather nice.

There are, sadly, exceptions that will only be detected at runtime, such as dividing by zero, trying to access elements in an array that don't exist, trying to reference an object with null, and other silly things. (These are generally termed *runtime exceptions*.)

The Throwable Class

There are two types of exceptions that both inherit from the Throwable class, shown in Figure 14-1: Error and Exception.

java.lang
Class Throwable

java.lang.Object
   └java.lang.Throwable

All Implemented Interfaces:
   Serializable

Direct Known Subclasses:
   Error, Exception

Figure 14-1. *The Throwable class*

I won't go into any detail on the Error class, but please read up on it yourself in the API documentation. Errors are fairly drastic problems, and no coding is going to get around an out-of-memory error. This is the *termination model*: program ends, game over.

We must, however, code for Exceptions—this is the *resumption model*, which allows the program to resume once the errors are dealt with.

Within the Exception subclasses, the RuntimeException does not have to be catered for—this is the exception to the rule (if you'll excuse the pun). The program will end with a rude message alerting the user about the runtime exception, but you are not forced to check for this type of exception. It should be said, however, that good programming techniques will usually do away with the need to check for these. In other words, check your array index yourself!

So enough of the boring theory, let's check out the practice. We'll look first at exception *handling* and then exception *throwing*.

Exception Handling

In cricket (here in England), we have a wicket keeper; in baseball there's a catcher. In either case, their job is to prevent the ball from going any further. In other words, they *catch* the ball. In Java, the thrown exception is the ball, and the try . . . catch block is the wicket keeper (or catcher).

The try . . . catch block

If we think that there is a possibility of an exception being thrown, we should wrap the code that could throw that exception in a try . . . catch block.

Let's look at an example that will also introduce you to some I/O. Don't panic, it's not that difficult. We'll read a character from the keyboard, and stop when the correct character has been pressed. Not rocket science, but it illustrates the point.

Incidentally, if you try to compile this code without putting it in a try . . . catch block, you would get an error something like this (the details depend on the JVM):

```
..\JavaBookExcept.java:25: unreported exception java.io.IOException; must be caught
or declared to be thrown.
```

As you can see, the exception must be caught. Let's look at the code:

```
/**
 * @(#)JavaBookExcept.java 1.1 07/15/05
 *
 * @author Alistair Rooney
 *
 * Basic Exception Handling Example
 * (c) Alistair Rooney 2005
 *
 * You may use this code, copy this code, sell this code,
 * print this code out and wallpaper your house with it
 * if you wish.
 **/

import java.io.*;
```

```java
class JavaBookExcept
{
    public static void main(String args[])
    {
        char castChar = ' ';
        System.out.println("Starting JavaBookExcept...");
        try
        {
            System.out.print("Please enter the letter 'a' : ");
            while (castChar != 'a')
            {
                castChar = (char)System.in.read();
            }
            System.out.println("\nWell Done, you typed "+castChar);
        }
        catch (IOException e)
        {
            System.err.println("\nAn Error was encountered :"+e);
        }
    }
}
```

What we've done here is attempted to execute the System.in.read method, and then we have asked the runtime to check if any IOExceptions were thrown. If any were, the runtime will *immediately* transfer execution to the catch block.

■**Note** This is important enough to repeat: The next line of code after the IOException is thrown will *not* execute. Execution is transferred to the catch block.

In its most basic sense, that's it! You now know how to handle exceptions. Please look up more about them, though. There is a lot more to exceptions than I can cover in this little introduction.

One thing I do need to cover before we leave the topic, though, is that you may have *more than one* catch block. If I wanted to catch an IOException and also a more general exception, I would just put the following additions into my code. I've marked them in bold so they're easy to see:

```java
/**
 * @(#)JavaBookExcept.java 1.0 03/10/18
 *
 * @author Alistair Rooney
 *
 * Basic Exception Handling Example
 * (c) Alistair Rooney 2003
 *
```

```
 * You may use this code, copy this code, sell this code,
 * print this code out and wallpaper your house with it
 * if you wish.
 **/

import java.io.*;

class JavaBookExcept
{
  public static void main(String args[])
  {
    char castChar = ' ';
    System.out.println("Starting JavaBookExcept...");
    try
    {
       System.out.print("Please enter the letter 'a' : ");
       while (castChar != 'a')
       {
          castChar = (char)System.in.read();
       }
       System.out.println("\nWell Done, you typed "+castChar);
    }
    catch (IOException e)
    {
       System.err.println("\nAn Error was encountered :"+e);
    }
    catch (Exception ex)
    {
       System.err.println("\nGeneral Exception :"+ex);
    }
  }
}
```

The finally block

One more thing before we move on to throwing exceptions: It is important to do some house-keeping when our method has completed. This, of course, needs to be done *whether an exception was caught or not*. The most elegant way of coding this is to use something called the finally block.

The finally block will *always* be executed. The syntax is very simple:

```
finally
{
    // Put some clean up code here.
}
```

Note Good programming style dictates that this block should be the last block in the whole `try` . . . `catch` . . . `finally` section.

Exception Throwing

Now that we know how to catch an exception, we can catch exceptions thrown either by standard Java or by other classes and methods that we are using. What if we want to throw our *own* exceptions?

We have two options: we can throw standard Java Exception classes (like IOException) or we can create our own Exception class and throw that. The latter is probably the best way to do things.

Tip If you use the second method, use an existing class that is similar to your Exception class and *extend* it. You don't have to do much. It would be sensible to use as much of the existing class as possible.

Let's create a new Exception, the FileMarkerException. It will be similar to the EOFException.

```
class FileMarkerException extends EOFException
{
    public FileMarkerException()
    {
    }

    public FileMarkerException(String s)
    {
        super(s);
    }
}
```

Not much to it, is there? All I've made sure of here is that I have two constructors identical to the superclass's ones. (Remember to check out the API documentation on the class you want to extend.)

There are two points you need to remember when you throw an exception.

- You must *instantiate* the exception (remember the new keyword).

- You must *advertise* the fact that you are throwing an exception in your method signature.

The syntax for both of these actions is as follows:

```
public void myThrowingMethod(File myFile) throws FileMarkerException
{
// some code here
  throw new FileMarkerException("Marker not found");
// some more code here
}
```

Notice the two areas in bold—they correspond to the two points made earlier. As you can see, throwing exceptions, whether your own or standard ones, is quite straightforward. Of course, if you use myThrowingMethod in another class, you would have to enclose it in a try . . . catch block!

An interesting final point here is that the client program can rethrow the exception. It can even change the nature of the exception.

If you wanted to merely rethrow the exception, you would do this:

```
catch (IOException e)
{
  throw e;
}
```

Or if you wanted to change the exception, you could do this:

```
catch (IOException e)
{
  throw new EOFException();
}
```

Before we leave the topic of exception handling, I need to emphasize one last point. In all of the preceding examples, you saw that we catch an exception and we give it a reference. For example, we might catch the IOException, as we did in the last example—and then give it the reference e. This means that we now have an *object reference* that we can use to access the methods of the Exception object.

The most common Exception methods we use are the utility methods getMessage, which will allow you to retrieve the text of the message, and printStackTrace, which will show you something akin to a "short dump" in ABAP.

Here's a very small, contrived example to illustrate this:

```
catch (IOException e)
    {
        System.err.println("Error: "+e.getMessage());
    }
```

That's the basics (and I do mean basics!) of exception handling and throwing. In the next lesson we'll discuss the feared topic of *threads*.

LESSON 15

■ ■ ■

Threads, Daemons, and Garbage Collection

ABAP does not have an accessible system of multi-threading, so I'm going to start this lesson by explaining a little about threads.

If I want a progress indicator in ABAP, I have to do some coding to "interrupt" my progress every so often, interrogate its status, and then feed this back to the progress indicator. This is a fine example of single threading.

It would be far more elegant to have the progress indicator interrogate the primary thread of the program without interrupting it. This is what we can do in Java by using separate threads. It's like having two programs on one session running at the same time.

■**Note** Even without using threads in Java, we have a least one thread running. This is what I call the primary thread. Our "Hello World" program in Lesson 1 had one thread running.

The subject of threads is potentially a little complex. Quite honestly, I think other topics are more complex (such as Enterprise JavaBeans), but this was such a concern for Sun that the topic of threads was left out of the original Java Certification Exam. As with any complex topic, take it slowly, code plenty of examples, and you will be fine. If you can, read other books on the subject, although for *this* topic I wouldn't recommend Bruce Eckel's book, as I find his examples cumbersome. Of course, that's just my opinion.

Since this is not meant to be a 700-page volume on Java, I will cover only the basics, but it should be enough to whet your appetite! I will cover simple threads, basic related threads, synchronized threads, and semaphoring threads. Then we can talk about daemon threads and the garbage collector.

Simple Threads

In Java, there are two ways we can define a thread class. We can extend the Thread class, or we can implement the interface Runnable. Sun recommends using Runnable, and I also recommend Runnable for various reasons that should become apparent. However, other Java pundits recommend Thread, so the choice is yours. I'll show an example of both.

```
/**
 *
 * @author Alistair Rooney
 *
 * Basic Threads Example
 * (c) Alistair Rooney 2003
 *
 *
 **/

class SimpleThread implements Runnable
{
    public void run()
    {
    // count from 1 to 10
        for(int i=1; i<11; i++)
        {
            System.out.println("i = "+i);
        }
    }
}
```

Simple enough, I think! Now we need something to run this—let's write a driver program. Remember, this class, SimplePrimary, will be the primary thread (although we don't see Thread or Runnable here).

```
/**
 *
 * @author Alistair Rooney
 *
 * Basic Threads Example
 * (c) Alistair Rooney 2003
 *
 *
 **/

 class SimplePrimary
{
    public static void main(String args[])
    {
        SimpleThread t = new SimpleThread();
        new Thread(t).start();
        // count from 1 to 10 again
        for(int x=1; x<11; x++)
        {
            System.out.println("x = "+x);
        }
    }
}
```

> **Tip** You will probably have noticed that we are instantiating a new Thread class in the preceding code. This needs to be done in order to execute the Runnable object.

What's happening here is that the SimplePrimary class counts x from 1 to 10, and just before it does this, it instantiates the SimpleThread class, which counts i from 1 to 10. All things being equal, SimpleThread should count from 1 to 10 before SimplePrimary (which is the primary thread). However the results are unpredictable, as you can see from the following output. It's important to note that these two threads are trying to run concurrently.

```
x = 1
i = 1
i = 2
i = 3
i = 4
i = 5
i = 6
i = 7
i = 8
i = 9
i = 10
x = 2
x = 3
x = 4
x = 5
x = 6
x = 7
x = 8
x = 9
x = 10
Press any key to continue...
```

To make these unrelated threads work more effectively, we could use the Thread.yield method in each. This makes each thread yield to one of equal *priority*. Have a look at the sidebar on thread priorities.

THREAD PRIORITIES

If you try to yield to a thread with a *lower* priority, the yield will be ignored. The yield method only works if all the threads are of equal priority. The default priority is generally 5, but the Thread class also provides us with constants to make this a little easier: NORM_PRIORITY is 5, MAX_PRIORITY is 10, and MIN_PRIORITY is 1.

The Thread class has a setPriority method to change the priority of the thread, and getPriority can be used to retrieve the priority.

Basic Related Threads

Have a look at the next two classes. What I've done is let different threads work on different sections of data. In this very trivial example, I'm asking each thread to count different sections in the range 1 to 100. Of course, in real life on a multiple-processor machine, such threads might be calculating prime numbers or something useful.

The "relation" that these threads share is that they are operating on the same group of data. Have a close look at the following code. I'm sure you'll be able to work out what's happening. What this shows is that unrelated threads can give some very unpredictable results.

```
/**
 *
 * @author Alistair Rooney
 *
 * Basic Related Threads Example
 * (c) Alistair Rooney 2003
 *
 *
 **/


class SimplePrimary
{
    public static void main(String args[])
    {
    int from = 1, to = 10;
        for (int i=1; i<5; i++)
        {
          new SimpleThread(from,to).start();
          from+=10;
          to+=10;
          System.out.println("Starting thread "+i);
        }
    }
}



/**
 *
 * @author Alistair Rooney
 *
 * Basic Threads Example
 * (c) Alistair Rooney 2003
 *
 *
 **/
```

```
class SimpleThread extends Thread
{
    int from;
    int to;

    SimpleThread(int from,int to)
    {
        this.from = from;
        this.to = to;
    }

 public void run()
    {
        System.out.println("Thread"+getName()+"Started");
        // count from 1 to 10 * Thread number
        for(int i=from; i<to+1; i++)
        {
            System.out.println("Thread "+getName()+"i = "+i);
        }
    yield();
    }
}
```

The beginning of the output will be something like this:

```
Starting thread 1
ThreadThread-1Started
Thread Thread-1i = 1
Thread Thread-1i = 2
Thread Thread-1i = 3
Thread Thread-1i = 4
Thread Thread-1i = 5
Thread Thread-1i = 6
Thread Thread-1i = 7
ThreadThread-2Started
Starting thread 2
Starting thread 3
Starting thread 4
Thread Thread-2i = 11
Thread Thread-2i = 12
Thread Thread-2i = 13
Thread Thread-2i = 14
Thread Thread-2i = 15
Thread Thread-1i = 8
ThreadThread-3Started
ThreadThread-4Started
Thread Thread-1i = 9
```

```
Thread Thread-3i = 21
Thread Thread-4i = 31
Thread Thread-1i = 10
Thread Thread-3i = 22
Thread Thread-4i = 32
Thread Thread-3i = 23
Thread Thread-4i = 33
Thread Thread-3i = 24
Thread Thread-2i = 16
Thread Thread-4i = 34
```

I've snipped the rest. Notice that there is *no real sequence* to these threads. They run in a fairly haphazard way. Take some time to review this code, run it yourself, and then improve on it. It could use some improvement!

Synchronized Threads

I want to show you a *simple* example of two methods accessing the same object and how we can *synchronize* their access. Look at the following code:

```
class Counter
{
    private int countVar;

    public synchronized int getCount()
    {
        return countVar;
    }

    public synchronized void incCount()
    {
        countVar+=1;
    }
}
```

Can you see what this is doing? It is allowing access to our data in a *managed* way. Many threads can now use this class and increment the counter in a truly synchronous way.

However, we still could have thread 1 incrementing the counter twice before thread 2 has even had a chance to run. We can manage this further by making use of a technique called *semaphoring*, which you will have come across before in your programming career.

Tip Since I am a Brit, I normally spell *synchronised* with an *s*. However, when you use synchronized in Java it *must* be spelled American-style with a *z*.

Semaphoring Threads

The technique of *semaphoring* involves using a "flag" (hence the name) to indicate whether or not the thread is allowed access or not. In other words, each thread can check to see if it is that thread's turn or not.

This is a good technique, but conventional thinking combines this with *wait pool* management. Think of the *wait pool* as a doctor's waiting room. When the doctor is ready to see you, the nurse (or *notifier*) will tell you that you can go in. After you have finished with the doctor, you will return to the wait pool until you are notified once again.

Let's see what this looks like in our code.

```
class Counter
{
    private int countVar;
    private boolean flag = false;

    public synchronized int getCount()
    {
        while (flag == false)
        {
            try
            {
                wait();
            }
            catch (InterruptedException e)
            {}
        }
        flag = false;
        notifyAll();
        return countVar;
    }

    public synchronized void incCount()
    {
        while (flag == true)
        {
            try
            {
                wait();
            }
            catch (InterruptedException e)
            {}
        }
```

```
        countVar+=1;
        flag = false;
        notifyAll();

    }
}
```

Try to work out what is happening here. In the getCount method, the thread is forced to wait if the flag is false. If it's true, the wait pool is notified, the flag is set to false, and the count is returned. If the incCount method is called while the flag is true, it will wait until notified.

We now have a pretty good system for controlling our threads. This combination of synchronizing, semaphoring, and wait pool management gives us something called *mutual exclusion*. No two threads will *ever* try to access the same data object.

Again, this subject is *large*, so I encourage you to explore threads further.

Daemon Threads and Garbage Collection

Daemon threads (pronounced *daymon*, not *demon*) are essentially low-priority threads that run in the background. The other main difference is that daemon threads do not necessarily have to belong to a particular program. In other words, you may shut down your program and find daemon threads still running. This makes a lot of sense if you think of these threads in terms of services.

The most well known daemon thread is the *garbage collector*. When Java creates an instance of an object, it allocates space on the heap for this new object. This is all well and dandy until the heap starts to fill up. If programs ended without cleaning up after themselves, we would soon run out of available memory.

In C we have to clean up manually, and forgetting to do this is a little too common, resulting in what we call *memory leaks*. In Java, however, an automatic service called the *garbage collector* runs and cleans up any unreferenced objects using the *mark and sweep* technique. (I'm not going to go into the different techniques here—those are for a software engineering course.)

The garbage collector can be called with the System.gc method, but it is important to note that this method acts only as a suggestion, and the garbage collector will run in its own sweet time!

To manually clean up your own objects, just set the object reference to null.

```
myRef = null;
```

Now that we know all about threads, we can start to look at the GUI features in standard Java: Swing in Lesson 16, event handling in Lesson 17, and AWT in Lesson 18.

■■■

Basic Swing Using Default Layouts

Now for some more interesting stuff—GUIs!

Admittedly, most of you will not code GUIs for applications. In the world of enterprise coding, it is becoming much less common for one developer to code both the business logic and the presentation logic. In the SAP world, your coding will mostly be JSPs, servlets, and EJBs.

However, you *should* know how to code presentation-side Java, and to do that these days we use Swing. (You may also want to look at SWT from Eclipse, http://www.eclipse.org.) In this short lesson we'll look at coding a few buttons on a panel.

■**Note** Swing is huge! I cannot possibly cover all the components in this introductory book. The good news is that once you know how to handle one component, the others are pretty easy. Remember to *read* the Java APIs.

In Swing we have a number of things called Containers. I am only going to cover two of these Containers, but remember to research the others. (You will only use these two 99 percent of the time, so don't panic.)

Containers

The root container that we will use is the JFrame. The JFrame cannot have components (Buttons, TextFields, and so on) put *directly* onto it. You must pass components to it via the ContentPane.

A discussion of the ContentPane is outside the scope of this book, but please have a look at Richard Baldwin's notes on the Internet (http://www.dickbaldwin.com/) if you have the time. For our purposes, we just need to remember to add our components to the JFrame via the ContentPane. I'll illustrate this in the code later.

What I normally do is add my components to a JPanel (this is my convention; it is not compulsory). Once I've done this, I add the JPanel to the JFrame. The JPanel is then a more manageable Container that I can position as I see fit.

A Simple Swing Example

Figure 16-1 shows the result we want to achieve. As you can see, this won't win any prizes for complexity!

Figure 16-1. *A simple Swing example*

This example is very easy to code. I've used two classes: SimpleSwing and SimplePanel. Remember that it's good practice to keep your classes in separate source files!

First we'll build our JPanel—here's the code for SimplePanel:

```
/**
*
* @author Alistair Rooney
*
* Simple Panel Example
* (c) Alistair Rooney 2005
*
*
**/

import javax.swing.*;

public class SimplePanel extends JPanel
{
public SimplePanel()
    {
        JButton button1 = new JButton("Button 1");
        JButton button2 = new JButton("Button 2");

        add(button1);
        add(button2);
    }
}
```

Notice the import statement. We need to access the swing package from the Java standard package. It is not part of the language section (java.lang), so we must import it.

Then the class extends a JPanel. If you recall inheritance, you'll know that this SimplePanel class is now a JPanel. It inherits all the methods of a JPanel, like the add method.

In the class's constructor we instantiate two JButtons and give them labels in their constructors. These labels will display on the front of the buttons. Then we simply add our two buttons to the JPanel (SimplePanel). Easy so far? I hope so.

Now that we have our completed JPanel, we need to pop it onto a JFrame and display the whole lot. Here's the code for our driver program, SimpleSwing.

```
/**
 *
 * @author Alistair Rooney
 *
 * Very Simple Swing Example
 * (c) Alistair Rooney 2005
 *
 *
 **/

import javax.swing.*;


class SimpleSwing extends JFrame
{

public static void main(String args[])
    {
        SimplePanel myPanel = new SimplePanel();
        SimpleSwing mainFrame = new SimpleSwing();
        mainFrame.setSize(200, 200);
        mainFrame.getContentPane().add(myPanel);
        mainFrame.setTitle("SimpleSwing");
        mainFrame.setVisible(true);
    }
}
```

Notice the import once again. And this time our class extends the JFrame class.

In the main method, we create an instance of the JPanel class, and we add it to the JFrame. (Incidentally, I do not approve of the "trick" technique of instantiating your own class in the main method, but I've done it here to keep things simple.) We now have a reference to our JFrame, called mainFrame.

Next, we set the size of the frame (200 pixels by 200 pixels) and then add the panel to the frame *via* the ContentPane. I've made this line bold to point out this technique.

We then set the title of the frame and make sure it is visible. Notice that by default a JFrame is not visible, so we must tell it to show itself. And that's it! You've completed your first Swing program.

There are two problems here, though:

1. We cannot close this JFrame down properly. If you click on the *X* button, it will hide the window, but the program will still be running.

2. The buttons are useless—they do nothing.

We will discuss these two issues in the next lesson, on event handling. Then, after we've covered event handling, we'll return to Swing to look at other components, and we'll also cover Layout sets. These are not SAPScript Layout sets, but Java Layout sets.

■ ■ ■

Event Handling

Java separates event handling and the GUI (either AWT or Swing). This separation is based on the *delegation model*, which is a model for event-driven programming. This is a very good thing for developers such as ourselves, since it allows us to change the GUI without affecting the event handling, and vice versa.

Event handling uses the original Abstract Window Toolkit (AWT) as explained in the sidebar. Since we need to use AWT to manage our events, we need to import AWT in our programs (as you will see when we look at some code).

It's also important to note that AWT has subpackages (or subdirectories if you like). In the case of event handling, we are interested in the *event* package, and I'll show you this in the code a little later.

Listening

I want to expand on our small example from Lesson 16, which displayed two buttons, to include the two points we identified earlier: we need to get the buttons to do something, and we need to allow the clicking of the *X* button at the top of the window to end the program. To do this, we need to employ interfaces called *listeners*.

To handle button clicks, we use the ActionListener interface. This requires that we implement its only method: `actionPerformed`.

We also have to use the WindowListener interface to close our window and end the program, but we have a slight problem here. We would have to implement seven methods! Fortunately, those nice folks at Sun have created a class that does the implementation. We can simply use this class, WindowAdapter, and just override the methods we require.

The most common way to deal with clicking the *X* button, though, is to use an anonymous class within our code. Let's have a look at the code to make this a bit clearer.

AWT AND SWING

Before JDK 1.1 you would have had to use AWT to draw buttons, labels, and so on. We can still use AWT, which takes advantage of some native Windows API calls but lacks the functionality found in Swing.

Swing was introduced with JDK 1.1.2 to *augment* but not replace AWT. As a result, AWT still contains the classes for two important parts of the GUI: event handling and the layout managers.

Note I have changed the button labels for this lesson.

```java
/**
 *
 * @author Alistair Rooney
 *
 * Simple Panel Example
 * (c) Alistair Rooney 2003
 *
 *
 **/

import javax.swing.*;
import java.awt.*;
import java.awt.event.*;


public class SimplePanel extends JPanel implements ActionListener
{
        JButton button1;
        JButton button2;

        public SimplePanel()
        {
            button1 = new JButton("Blue");
            button2 = new JButton("Red");

            add(button1);
            add(button2);

            button1.addActionListener(this);
            button2.addActionListener(this);
        }

        public void actionPerformed(ActionEvent ae)
        {
            Object button = ae.getSource();
            Color color = getBackground();
            if (button == button1)
            {
                color = Color.blue;
            }
            if (button == button2)
            {
                color = Color.red;
```

```
        }
        setBackground(color);
        repaint();
    }
}
```

The driver class, SimpleSwing, has not changed yet, but as you can see, I've implemented our ActionListener and overridden the actionPerformed method, which will be run automatically when a button is clicked. Notice how I have added an ActionListener to each button. Which ActionListener? This one, hence the keyword this.

The actionPerformed method examines the ActionEvent object being passed and deduces whether the "Red" button or the "Blue" button has been clicked. It then sets the background color and repaints the screen (sometimes this is not necessary, but it's better to be safe).

Also notice my new import at the top, java.awt.event.*, which allows me to use these event handling classes.

If you key this code in and run it, you should see the window shown in Figure 17-1.

Figure 17-1. *Handling our events*

We've managed to put some event handling code on our buttons! Is this cool or what? But hang on, we've forgotten something. We still need to put a WindowListener on our JFrame, so that we can control the window closing. Let's have a peep at the code:

```
/**
 *
 * @author Alistair Rooney
 *
 * Very Simple Swing Example
 * (c) Alistair Rooney 2003
 *
 *
 **/

import javax.swing.*;
import java.awt.event.*;


class SimpleSwing extends JFrame
{
```

```
public static void main(String args[])
{
    SimplePanel myPanel = new SimplePanel();
    SimpleSwing mainFrame = new SimpleSwing();
    mainFrame.setSize(200, 200);
    mainFrame.addWindowListener(new WindowAdapter()
    {
        public void windowClosing(WindowEvent e)
        {
            System.exit(0);
        }
    }
    );
    mainFrame.getContentPane().add(myPanel);
    mainFrame.setTitle("SimpleSwing");
    mainFrame.setVisible(true);
}
}
```

Notice that the only change I have made in this code is to use an anonymous class (WindowAdapter) to manage the window closing. If you click on the *X* button now, the window will close and System.exit(0) will end my program elegantly.

■**Tip** There are plenty of other listeners. Check out the APIs in the Java documentation.

That's all for this lesson, folks! Next we will look at layout managers so that we can control where our components go. We'll also look at some more of the 300-odd classes within Swing.

■ ■ ■

Layout Managers and Other Components

A layout manager looks after the placement of the Swing or AWT components in a container. In Lesson 16 we saw a JPanel and a JFrame. Both of these are containers, and they both have default layout managers.

The default layout manager for a JPanel is FlowLayout, so let's start with it. We've already used it without realizing it in Lesson 16.

We will also explore some other Swing components in this lesson.

FlowLayout

When we added the buttons to the JPanel in our example in Lesson 16, we used the FlowLayout layout manager, since it is the default. Unless you specify otherwise, FlowLayout will start by placing components in the center and then spread outwards, attempting to keep the components centered at all times.

You can, of course, make it fill from the left or right by using the FlowLayout.LEFT or FlowLayout.RIGHT constants.

If you use the FlowLayout class, you must import java.awt.FlowLayout, or, if you prefer, java.awt.* (if you are using many classes from the awt package).

We've already seen FlowLayout in action, so I won't bore you with another example, but Figure 18-1 shows an example.

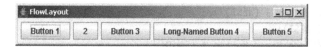

Figure 18-1. *FlowLayout in an applet window*

BorderLayout

BorderLayout is one of the most versatile layout managers. It also happens to be the default layout for a JFrame. (To be more accurate, it is the default for a ContentPane, but it's permissible to think of it as the default for a JFrame.)

BorderLayout allows you to position components or other containers in one of five general areas: NORTH, SOUTH, EAST, WEST, and CENTER. Figure 18-2 shows an example of a BorderLayout object.

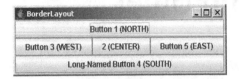

Figure 18-2. *BorderLayout in an applet window*

Here's the program that generates this window:

```
/*
 * Swing version.
 */

import java.awt.*;
import java.awt.event.*;
import javax.swing.*;

public class BorderWindow extends JFrame
  {
    boolean inAnApplet = true;

    public BorderWindow()
      {
        Container contentPane = getContentPane();
        //Use the content pane's default BorderLayout.
        //contentPane.setLayout(new BorderLayout()); //unnecessary

        contentPane.add(new JButton("Button 1 (NORTH)"),
                    BorderLayout.NORTH);
        contentPane.add(new JButton("2 (CENTER)"),
                    BorderLayout.CENTER);
        contentPane.add(new JButton("Button 3 (WEST)"),
                    BorderLayout.WEST);
        contentPane.add(new JButton("Long-Named Button 4 (SOUTH)"),
                    BorderLayout.SOUTH);
        contentPane.add(new JButton("Button 5 (EAST)"),
                    BorderLayout.EAST);

        addWindowListener(new WindowAdapter()
          {
            public void windowClosing(WindowEvent e)
              {
                if (inAnApplet)
```

```
                {
                    dispose();
                } else
                {
                    System.exit(0);
                }
            }
        });
    }

    public static void main(String args[])
    {
        BorderWindow window = new BorderWindow();
        window.inAnApplet = false;

        window.setTitle("BorderLayout");
        window.pack();
        window.setVisible(true);
    }
}
```

I've put the important part in bold. Don't waste time worrying about things like `inAnApplet`. I won't be covering applets in this book, but feel free to research them on your own. You can start at Sun's site: `http://java.sun.com`.

GridLayout

The last layout manager I will cover is the GridLayout. (There are many more layout managers that you should research.) Again, this is quite easy to code. Figure 18-3 shows an example.

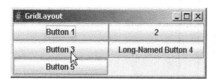

Figure 18-3. *GridLayout in an applet window*

As you can see in the figure, we have a grid with two columns and three rows. You can set the grid dimensions in the GridLayout constructor:

```
contentPane.setLayout(new GridLayout(0,2));

contentPane.add(new JButton("Button 1"));
contentPane.add(new JButton("2"));
contentPane.add(new JButton("Button 3"));
contentPane.add(new JButton("Long-Named Button 4"));
contentPane.add(new JButton("Button 5"));
```

The interesting point is that the constructor specifies 0 rows and 2 columns, yet we see three rows in the running applet. The value 0 tells the runtime to use *as many rows as necessary*, and in this example that happened to be three.

Of course, we could have coded 3 as well, like this:

```
contentPane.setLayout(new GridLayout(3,2));
```

It will do exactly the same thing.

■**Note** The most important thing about building a GUI is that you should *plan* your design ahead of time. This may seem obvious, but it's surprising how many people try to "wing it."

Layout Design Example

In this design example, we want to produce a calculator. There are many different ways of doing this, and I'll put forward just *one* possibility.

The first thing we need to do is sketch the finished product and then work out how we will create this result using components and containers. My sketch is shown in Figure 18-4.

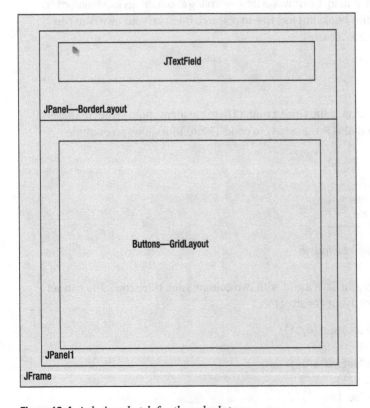

Figure 18-4. *A design sketch for the calculator*

As you may be able to see from my design, I have my JFrame container holding two JPanels:

- The upper or NORTH JPanel will hold the calculator's display. A BorderLayout can be used here, since one of the characteristics of this layout is that it will allow the component (in this case a JTextField) to fill all the available space.

- The CENTER JPanel will hold the buttons, and I think you'll agree that a GridLayout will be appropriate here.

I hope you will try to code this calculator as a test of all the skills you've learned so far. It should keep you busy for an evening or two!

Other Atomic Components

Let's quickly go through some of the more common atomic components you may use on a GUI. The most common two components (apart from the JButton) are the JLabel and the JTextField.

Suppose we want to achieve the result shown in Figure 18-5. The JLabel will produce the label to the left ("Please Enter the Code") and the JTextField will present the user with a text box to enter data.

Figure 18-5. *Creating labels and text fields*

You can use the JTextField.setText method to put a value into the field and JTextField.getText to retrieve text from the field. You can even use a listener on the text field if you need to, but it is not usually necessary.

Here's the code for the example above. First the JFrame:

```
/**
 *
 * @author Alistair Rooney
 *
 * Very Simple Swing Example
 * (c) Alistair Rooney 2003
 *
 *
 **/
```

```java
import javax.swing.*;
import java.awt.event.*;
import java.awt.*;


class JCompmain extends JFrame
{

    public static void main(String args[])
    {
        JComponents myPanel = new JComponents();
        JCompmain mainFrame = new JCompmain();
        mainFrame.setSize(200, 200);
        mainFrame.addWindowListener(new WindowAdapter()
            {
                public void windowClosing(WindowEvent e)
                {
                    System.exit(0);
                }
            }
            );
        mainFrame.getContentPane().add(myPanel, BorderLayout.NORTH);
        mainFrame.setTitle("JComponents");
        mainFrame.setVisible(true);
    }
}
```

Note that I have placed the NORTH JPanel on the JFrame. This is a technique to constrain it in a narrow band for aesthetic reasons.

Now the JPanel:

```java
/**
 *
 * @author Alistair Rooney
 *
 * Simple Panel Example
 * (c) Alistair Rooney 2003
 *
 *
 **/

import javax.swing.*;
import java.awt.*;
```

```
public class JComponents extends JPanel
{
    JLabel label;
    JTextField text;

    public JComponents()
    {
    setLayout(new BorderLayout());
    label = new JLabel("Please Enter the Code");
    text = new JTextField();

    add(label, BorderLayout.WEST);
    add(text, BorderLayout.CENTER);

    }
}
```

This should be clear.

This ends Part 1 of the book! The next part focuses on some essential topics that make up Enterprise Java. These include servlets, JDBC, Java messaging, XML, JSP, and even an intro to EJB 3.0.

Please bear in mind that I have just scratched the surface here. Make use of Sun's tutorials, which you can find at http://java.sun.com.

PART 2

■■■

Enterprise Java

In the second part of this book, we will explore the essential topics for enterprise development. When developing enterprise applications, we must always be mindful of three separate areas: the database, the presentation logic, and the business logic. However, there is one more area that, in this era of increasing system integration, is becoming more important: messaging. In the case of Java and NetWeaver, this is the Java Message Service. We will also scratch the surface of Enterprise JavaBeans 3.0.

In this part of the book, you can pick and choose the lessons you want to cover, but be aware that most are interdependent.

LESSON 19

■■■

JDBC Technology

Java Database Connectivity (JDBC) is the standard way to connect to an external database from Java. It uses Structured Query Language (SQL) to access and update the database.

It should be stressed that this is not the *only* way to access a database. For example, the IBM AS/400 (iSeries) has an implementation of Java that allows direct database access through nonstandard IBM APIs. The benefit of this method is that the database access is incredibly quick (the AS/400 consistently comes out on top as the world's fastest transaction server), and it takes advantage of the native database functionality. The drawback is that this approach sacrifices the "write once, run anywhere" ethos.

JDBC Drivers

JDBC drivers allow the Java programmer to communicate with a database management system (DBMS). Although some basic drivers are delivered with Java, DBMS vendors supply JDBC drivers with their systems. These drivers fall into four basic types.

In SAP-land, we have other mechanisms for talking to databases, but Exchange Infrastructure 3.0 can happily use JDBC.

Type 1 Drivers

Type 1 JDBC drivers are also known as *bridge drivers*, such as the JDBC-ODBC bridge driver. These drivers rely on an intermediary, such as ODBC, to transfer the SQL calls to the database. Bridge drivers often rely on native code, although the JDBC-ODBC library native code is part of the Java 5 Virtual Machine. It is widely believed that these drivers are much slower than others, and they are avoided for this reason. Interestingly enough, recent studies have shown them to be as quick, and sometimes *quicker*, than other drivers.

These are the drivers we will use in our examples, but please experiment with the other drivers on your own.

Type 2 Drivers

Type 2 drivers use the existing database API to communicate with the database on the client. Although Type 2 drivers are generally considered faster than Type 1 drivers, Type 2 drivers use native code and require additional permissions to work in an applet.

A Type 2 driver might need client-side database code to connect over the network.

Type 3 Drivers

Type 3 drivers call the database API on the server. JDBC requests from the client are first prox-ied to the JDBC driver on the server to run. Type 3 and 4 drivers can be used by thin clients, as they need no native code.

Type 4 Drivers

The highest level of driver re-implements the database network API in the Java language. Type 4 drivers can also be used on thin clients, as they have no native code.

Loading the Driver

The first step you need to complete before connecting to a database is to load the driver. To do this, we use the `class.forName` method.

Here's how we would load the JDBC-ODBC bridge driver (which comes with the Java SDK):

```
Class.forName("sun.jdbc.odbc.JdbcOdbcDriver");
```

It's a bit long-winded, but we just need to do it once per application.

Remember to put this in a `try . . . catch` block to take care of any exceptions that may be thrown.

Note There is another more manual way of loading the JDBC driver, but this technique is used by nearly all Java programmers.

Connecting to the Database

Since we will be looking at the JDBC-ODBC driver in our examples, you will need to know how to set up an ODBC connection. I have several in my Windows ODBC Data Sources window, as you can see in Figure 19-1.

To access this, click on Administrative Tools in your Control Panel (Windows 2000 or XP). After that, click on Data Sources (ODBC), and you should see something like Figure 19-1. From here you can add, change, or delete your data sources.

Note The important point here is that the name of the data source in the ODBC Data Source Administrator window is the name you will use in your program.

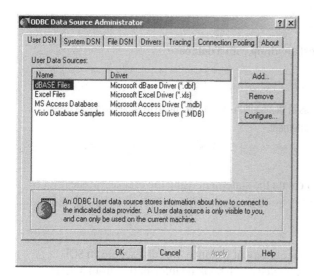

Figure 19-1. *ODBC data sources*

Now we can code our URL to the data source or database. We first define our URL, which must follow the format jdbc:odbc:xxxxx (where xxxxx is the name of your data source) if we are using the JDBC-ODBC bridge. (If you are using a JDBC driver provided by a third party, don't fret—the URL for the driver is normally well documented.)

Once we've done that, we can use the URL to connect by calling the getConnection method in our DriverManager class. Easy, no? Here's an example:

```
String myURL = "jdbc:odbc:userControl";
myCon = DriverManager.getConnection(myURL, "","");
```

Don't forget to close your connection when you've finished with the database. Here's an example:

```
myCon.close();
```

Once we have our connection, we can concentrate on building a Statement.

Note The JDBC classes—Connection, Statement, DriverManager, and so on—live in the SQL package, which must be imported before we can use it. The code samples later in this lesson show how we do this in Java.

Creating Statements

With the Statement class, we can do almost anything with a database.

▰**Tip** We will be focusing on the Statement class in this section, but I urge you to examine two subclasses of Statement: CallableStatement and PreparedStatement.

Let's examine a simple insert. We first create the statement using the `createStatement` method in the Connection class instance:

```
myStat = myCon.createStatement();
```

This is good so far. Now that we have our Statement instance, we can execute an SQL string. For this example, imagine we have extracted some booking information from a user interface—we are going to add this information as a record to a table in our database. The Table name is `registration`.

Here's how we do this:

```
myStat.execute("INSERT INTO registration (FirstName, LastName, Salutation, email, "+
          "RoomType) VALUES ("+ guestData +");");
```

Don't forget to close the Statement once you've used it. (This is *not* the same as closing the Connection.)

```
myStat.close();
```

Now that we've examined the basics of a table insert, let's see all the code together. I've included a snippet from a Servlet class I use for training, but please don't worry about the Servlet code. I've made the important bits bold, and I've chopped chunks out of this program, to make it more readable.

STRUCTURED QUERY LANGUAGE

When Messrs. Boyce and Codd from IBM developed the relational database, they also decided to develop a natural English-style interface to those relational databases. Thus, SQL was born. SQL stands for Structured Query Language and is *not* pronounced "Sequel"—that pronunciation is for a database product from Microsoft, which is not the same thing at all. I have made the assumption here that you are already familiar with SQL from your ABAP coding.

```
/*
 * 3-Tier Java example (NOT the Full program!)
 *
 *
 */

import java.io.*;
import java.sql.*;
import javax.servlet.*;
import javax.servlet.http.*;
import java.util.*;
import javax.mail.*;
import javax.mail.internet.*;
/**
 *
 * @author Alistair Rooney
 */
public class GuestReservation extends HttpServlet
{
    private Statement myStat = null;
    private Connection myCon = null;

    public void init(ServletConfig config) throws ServletException
    {
        super.init(config);
        try
        {
            Class.forName("sun.jdbc.odbc.JdbcOdbcDriver");
            String myURL = "jdbc:odbc:Guest";
            myCon = DriverManager.getConnection(myURL, "","");
        }
        catch(Exception e)
        {
            e.printStackTrace();
            System.err.println("ERROR: Cannot create a Connection");
            myCon = null;
        }
}

public void doPost(HttpServletRequest req, HttpServletResponse res)
        throws ServletException, IOException
```

```
. . .
//code snipped out that will call submitData, handle HTML, etc.
. . .

private boolean submitData(String guestData)
      {
          try
          {
            myStat = myCon.createStatement();
            myStat.execute("INSERT INTO registration (FirstName, LastName,
            Salutation, email, "+"RoomType) VALUES ("+ guestData +");");
            myStat.close();
            return true;
          }
          catch(Exception ex)
          {
              System.err.println("ERROR: Cannot enter guest into database");
              ex.printStackTrace();
              return false;
          }
      }

      public void destroy()
      {
          try
          {
             myCon.close();
          }
          catch(Exception ex)
          {
              System.err.println("ERROR: Cannot CLOSE database");
          }
      }

}
```

Notice that I've put everything into try . . . catch blocks for decent exception handling. Updates can also be done using the executeUpdate method.

■**Note** Please be aware that although Java can use some advanced features, the underlying database may not support those features. For example, there is little point trying to get too clever with an Access DBMS, since it is a very simple stand-alone database with limited functionality. On the other hand, you would proba-bly have no problems with Oracle or DB/2, which are enterprise-ready full-function database management systems.

ResultSets

Think of a ResultSet as being much like an internal table in ABAP. It is a workable storage area within program memory that stores the results from a select statement.

One of the most exciting features of JDBC is the ResultSet class's methods for processing the results. Now would be a very good time for you to review the method summary in the API documentation under the ResultSet class.

First let's look at some simple code that connects to a database, runs an SQL query, and returns the results in a ResultSet:

```java
import java.sql.*;

public class InsertUser
{
    public static void main(String args[])
    {
        Connection myCon;
        try
        {
            Class.forName("sun.jdbc.odbc.JdbcOdbcDriver");
        }
            catch (Exception ex)
        {
            System.err.println("No DRIVER loaded! "+ ex);
            return;
        }
        try
        {
            String theURL = "jdbc:odbc:MiniClinic";
            myCon = DriverManager.getConnection(theURL," ", " ");
        }
        catch (Exception e)
        {
            System.err.println("No CONNECTION dude! "+ e);
            return;
        }

        try
        {
            Statement myStmt = myCon.createStatement();
            ResultSet rs = myStmt.executeQuery("SELECT * FROM USER");

            while(rs.next())
            {
                int acode = rs.getInt("aCode");
                String userName = rs.getString("userName");
                int passw = rs.getInt("password");
                System.out.println("User is: "+acode+" "+userName+" "+passw);
```

```
            }
        }
        catch (Exception es)
        {
            System.err.println("SQL Problem! "+ es);
        }
        finally
        {
            try
            {
                myCon.close();
                return;
            }
            catch(Exception e)
            {}
        }
    }
}
```

Can you see what's happening here? You should be OK until the point where we do the executeQuery. If you have a look at the method in the APIs, you'll see that it returns a ResultSet object. Think of this whole action as being similar to an Array Fetch in ABAP. As I mentioned earlier, you can think of the ResultSet as being like an internal table—they are very similar conceptually. What we have done is pulled in every record from the table User in my MiniClinic database.

Now this is the important part: The next method in ResultSet does two things. It will return a true or false boolean value depending on whether there are more records in the ResultSet or not. If there are more records, it will move the cursor to the next record. A cursor is a pointer, very like the sy-tabix variable in ABAP. If there were no records returned, the method would return false. This is quite useful, because we can use this in a while loop, as you can see in the code. Incidentally, the cursor is initially positioned just *before* the first record, not on it.

In the while loop, we see three variables getting loaded. An integer acode, a String userName, and an integer passw.

Now we use the relevant method in ResultSet to extract the data. To do this, you must know the field names in the database table, since that is how we refer to them. As you can see from the code, we load acode, userName, and passw into variables using getInt and getString. We then print them out using our good old System.out method. In the finally block (remember those?) we close the connection.

Figure 19-2 shows the output I had from my run:

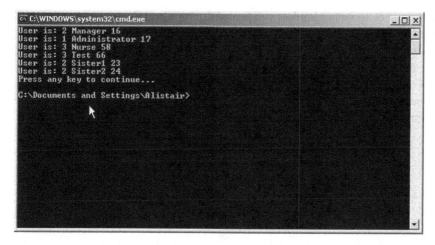

Figure 19-2. *Results from the JDBC program*

With the right class of driver (and the right database) we can go forwards and backwards through the ResultSet. We can position the cursor at an absolute row number with the absolute method, or move the cursor relative to a row with the relative method.

I mentioned earlier that the ResultSet is similar to an internal table in ABAP, but we haven't seen how to delete, modify, or insert rows yet.

To update, move your cursor to the correct row and then use the updateInt method or the respective method for your field type. Once you have updated the fields, you *must* call the updateRow method to update the underlying database. If you don't, your changes will be lost.

To delete a row, position your cursor (carefully!) and call deleteRow.

Inserting a row is a little more tricky. You must first move the cursor to the insert row (much like the Header line in ABAP). To do this, use this method:

```
rs.moveToInsertRow();
```

You can then updatexxx your fields (where xxx is the primitive data type) and refer to them by name (or position) and the new value. If you specify by position, notice that field numbers start with 1 and not with 0, as do most other things in Java. It is nicer to use the names, though. Here's an example:

```
rs.updateInt("aCode", 3);
rs.updateString("userName", "Mary Poppins");
rs.getInt("password", 378);
```

Then you can do an insertRow to put it into the database:

```
rs.insertRow();
```

That wraps up ResultSet updates. I implore you to read the section at the top of the ResultSet API documentation. It lays out what is required to have a scrollable, updateable result set. Also, explore the getMetaData method for really professional code, and the PreparedStatement and CallableStatement classes.

Entire books have been written on JDBC, and I hope this little introduction to the basics has made you enthusiastic about reading more.

In the next lesson I'm going to talk about SAP's Java Connector.

■ ■ ■

The Java Connector (JCo)

JCo is a set of classes (separately downloadable from http://service.sap.com) that allow Java programs to connect to SAP systems and invoke Remote Function Modules. It also allows parsing of IDocs (SAP Intermediate Documents) amongst other things.

I will only be dealing with Java-to-RFC calls in this lesson, but ABAP can call Java too! The example I will use is a refinement of an example delivered with JCo. It is very contrived and would not really be useful in a live environment, but it will give you an example of how to use most things in JCo.

Downloading and Installing JCo

You must be an SAP customer to download JCo. Use your OSS login and download it from http://service.sap.com/connectors. I used version 2.1.1 on a Windows XP machine, but you should find versions available for Linux and other platforms. It uses the Java Native Interface (JNI; read up on this!) so it is platform specific.

Once you have downloaded the zip file, I recommend unzipping it into the C:\JCo directory to keep things simple.

Note Make sure you copy librfc32.dll from the JCo directory to your C:\...\system32 directory. On my machine, this is C:\WINDOWS\system32, but it will be different depending on your Windows platform.

You must have jco.jar in your class path when running your project.

A JCo Example

This is a variation on one of the examples provided with JCo. I've made a change to export the results from the BAPI to a JTable, and I've left the detailed output to list to the console. This isn't very exciting, but it will give you a good skeleton program to base your BAPI calls upon.

The code is long, but *don't panic!* I'll explain everything, piece by piece.

```java
import com.sap.mw.jco.*;
//import java.util.*;

/**
 * @author Alistair Rooney
 *
 * Execute the BAPI to fetch the Companies from SAP
 * Alistair Rooney (c) 2002 2003
 *
 */
public class TestSAPBAPI
{

  JCO.Client mConnection;
  JCO.Repository mRepository;


  public TestSAPBAPI()
  {
    Object[] [] data;
    try
    {
    // Change the logon information to your own system/user
      mConnection =
      JCO.createClient("005", // SAP client
      "arooney",              // userid
      "********",             // password (Fill in your real password)
      null,                   // language
      "Goofy",                // application server host name
      "00");                  // system number
      mConnection.connect();
      mRepository = new JCO.Repository("ARAsoft", mConnection);
    }
    catch (Exception ex)
    {
      ex.printStackTrace();
      System.exit(1);
    }
    JCO.Function function = null;
    JCO.Table codes = null;
    try
    {
      function = this.createFunction("BAPI_COMPANYCODE_GETLIST");
      if (function == null)
      {
        System.out.println("BAPI_COMPANYCODE_GETLIST" +
```

```
                              " not found in SAP.");
      System.exit(1);
   }
   mConnection.execute(function);
   JCO.Structure returnStructure =
      function.getExportParameterList().getStructure("RETURN");
   if (! (returnStructure.getString("TYPE").equals("") ||
          returnStructure.getString("TYPE").equals("S")) )
   {
      System.out.println(returnStructure.getString("MESSAGE"));
      System.exit(1);
   }
   codes =
      function.getTableParameterList().getTable("COMPANYCODE_LIST");
   data = new Object[codes.getNumRows()] [2];
   for (int i = 0; i < codes.getNumRows(); i++)
   {
      codes.setRow(i);
      data[i][0] = codes.getString("COMP_CODE");
      data[i][1] = codes.getString("COMP_NAME");
   }
   DisplayFrame df = new DisplayFrame(data);
}
catch (Exception ex)
{
   ex.printStackTrace();
   System.exit(1);
}
try
{
   codes.firstRow();
   for (int i = 0; i < codes.getNumRows(); i++, codes.nextRow())
    {
      function = this.createFunction("BAPI_COMPANYCODE_GETDETAIL");
      if (function == null)
      {
        System.out.println("BAPI_COMPANYCODE_GETDETAIL" +
                          " not found in SAP.");
        System.exit(1);
      }
      function.getImportParameterList().
        setValue(codes.getString("COMP_CODE"), "COMPANYCODEID");
      function.getExportParameterList().setActive(false, "COMPANYCODE_ADDRESS");
      mConnection.execute(function);
      JCO.Structure returnStructure =
        function.getExportParameterList().getStructure("RETURN");
      if (! (returnStructure.getString("TYPE").equals("") ||
```

```
                    returnStructure.getString("TYPE").equals("S") ||
                    returnStructure.getString("TYPE").equals("W")) )
        {
          System.out.println(returnStructure.getString("MESSAGE"));
        }
        JCO.Structure detail =
          function.getExportParameterList().
          getStructure("COMPANYCODE_DETAIL");
          System.out.println(detail.getString("COMP_CODE") + '\t' +
          detail.getString("COUNTRY") + '\t' +
          detail.getString("CHRT_ACCTS") + '\t' +
          detail.getString("CITY"));
      }

  }
  catch (Exception ex)
  {
    ex.printStackTrace();
    System.exit(1);
  }
  finally
  {
    mConnection.disconnect();
  }
}
public JCO.Function createFunction(String name) throws Exception
{
  try
  {
    IFunctionTemplate ft = mRepository.getFunctionTemplate(name.toUpperCase());
    if (ft == null)
      return null;
    return ft.getFunction();
  }
  catch (Exception ex)
  {
    throw new Exception("Problem retrieving JCO.Function object.");
  }
}
public static void main (String args[])
{
  TestSAPBAPI app = new TestSAPBAPI();
}
}
```

I have only listed the main program here. I will list the JFrame and JPanel code at the end of this lesson for your interest.

The first thing you need to notice is the `import` statement. We are obviously importing JCo so that we can use the classes. (JCo comes with its own API documentation—please review it!).

In this program I have followed the JCo example and put the `main` method at the end of the code.

The constructor contains a two-dimensional array called `data`, which we use to populate the JTable. Then we open a `try . . . catch` block and try to build a connection by using the `createClient` method from the `JCO` class. We need to give it all the parameters we would normally give to the SAP logon program. I have put stars in the password field because I don't want you seeing my password! Obviously you would replace the values in my code with your own values.

Once we have created a client, we merely connect using the `connect` method from the newly built client (called `mConnection` here).

The next thing we need to do is nominate a repository (yes, just like your normal SAP repository) to use for your Java program. This is pretty cool, because we then have access to any items in your repository.

We will only use one repository here, but as you can see, we can name it using a String. I've called the repository object `mRepository`.

We then declare our Function and Table classes and assign them a variable. The Function will point to our BAPI, and our Table will be the internal table we return from the BAPI. Excited yet? Internal tables in Java!

Next we need to create a function that uses the BAPI `BAPI_COMPANYCODE_GETLIST`. We do this by using the `createFunction` method and then executing this function by using the `mConnection.execute` method and passing our function as a parameter.

In the next line of code, we create a structure based on the export structure from our BAPI. I've called this `returnStructure`.

Next, we define our `codes` table and populate it from the BAPI, we build a two-dimensional array based on the size of the internal table, and we cycle through our internal table populating our array to put into the JTable. We then create an instance of the Frame class and pass it the array.

You should get something like the table shown in Figure 20-1 (depending on the company codes in your system).

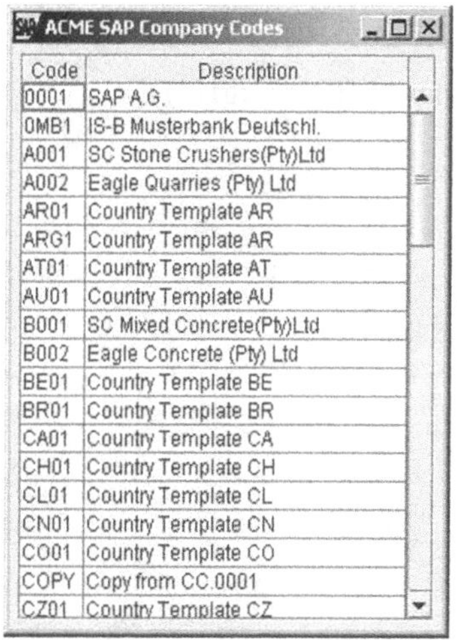

Code	Description
0001	SAP A.G.
OMB1	IS-B Musterbank Deutschl.
A001	SC Stone Crushers(Pty)Ltd
A002	Eagle Quarries (Pty) Ltd
AR01	Country Template AR
ARG1	Country Template AR
AT01	Country Template AT
AU01	Country Template AU
B001	SC Mixed Concrete(Pty)Ltd
B002	Eagle Concrete (Pty) Ltd
BE01	Country Template BE
BR01	Country Template BR
CA01	Country Template CA
CH01	Country Template CH
CL01	Country Template CL
CN01	Country Template CN
CO01	Country Template CO
COPY	Copy from CC.0001
CZ01	Country Template CZ

Figure 20-1. *Company codes JTable*

The next section of code displays the details for each of these company codes in the console. We do this by creating a function linked to the BAPI_COMPANYCODE_GETDETAIL. The coding is almost identical to the previous section, from a technical point of view, so I won't bore you by going through it. Notice, though, that I have selected the company code, country, chart of accounts, and city fields to be reported.

Note Notice in the JFrame code below I have used my own little icon to replace the standard icon that Java uses in the top-left corner. You will have to comment the code out to run this program, or develop your own little (50 × 50 pixels) icon.

Here is the code for the two remaining classes:

```java
import javax.swing.*;
import java.awt.*;
import java.awt.event.*;
//import java.util.*;

/**
 * @author Alistair Rooney
 * @version 1.0
 * Copyright 2002 2003 All rights reserved
 *
 * Example program using the SAP Java Connector to display company codes
 */
public class DisplayFrame extends JFrame
{
    public DisplayFrame(Object[] [] data)
    {
        DisplayPanel panel = new DisplayPanel(data);
        setTitle("My Company SAP Company Codes");
        Toolkit tk = Toolkit.getDefaultToolkit();
        setIconImage(tk.createImage(DisplayFrame.class.getResource("MyIcon.gif")));

        addWindowListener(new WindowAdapter()
        {
            public void windowClosing(WindowEvent e)
            {
                System.exit(0);
            }
        }
        );
        getContentPane().add(panel);
        pack();
        setVisible(true);
    }
```

```java
}


//import java.awt.event.ActionListener;
import java.util.*;
import java.awt.*;
import javax.swing.*;
import javax.swing.table.*;

/**
 * @author Alistair Rooney
 *
 * Panel to contain the load button and JTable to
 * view the SAP company codes.
 *
 * All rights reserved (c) 2002 2003
 */
public class DisplayPanel extends JPanel
{
    JTable table;
    Vector names;

    public DisplayPanel(Object [] [] data)
    {
        Object[] names = {"Code","Description"};
        table = new JTable(data, names);
        // add to table.
        TableColumn column = null;
        for (int i = 0; i < 2; i++)
        {
          column = table.getColumnModel().getColumn(i);
          if (i == 0)
          {
          // "Company codes" is small
            column.setPreferredWidth(40);
          }
          else
          {
            column.setPreferredWidth(200);
          }
}

        JScrollPane scrollPane = new JScrollPane(table);
        table.setPreferredScrollableViewportSize(new Dimension(240, 300));
        add(scrollPane);
    }

}
```

There is some new Java functionality here that you won't have seen before, but try to work through it. ScrollPanes and JTables are both very useful Swing components.

That concludes a very basic introduction to JCo.

Tip Thomas G. Schuessler from ARASoft (`http://www.arasoft.de`) will be publishing a book on JCo and the new IDoc library that will be very useful if you intend to use the JCo—JCo is fantastic at reading and writing IDocs.

The next lesson is servlets!

LESSON 21

■■■

Servlets

Way back in 1995, at the very first JavaOne conference in San Francisco, the Java team (James Gosling and friends) showed that we could have animation in a web page. The Web was very young at the time, and this really was a very new and exciting development. The mechanism used to present these animations were called *applets*.

We won't cover applets in this book—applets have a few drawbacks, and they've now largely drifted into the history of Java. One of the most severe drawbacks was that you had to download the applet from the server every time you navigated to the web site. This meant extra time that, even in this day of broadband, a client is not willing to spend.

So enter *servlets*. Servlets run on the server, so they don't tie up client resources, and they can also access databases. (This was demonstrated in Lesson 19 in an example of a three-tier application—presentation, application, and database tiers.) Servlets are also very easy to code!

Hypertext Transfer Protocol

HTTP is very important when we use servlets, because this is the protocol we will use to communicate between our client and our server.

If we think in terms of a web browser and a web server (see Figure 21-1) we can see that the browser initiates a request, and the server replies with a response. We call this the request/response model. Clearly there is a lot more to HTTP than this, but it's not really within the scope of this book.

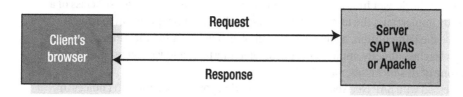

Figure 21-1. *The request/response model*

That's the broad overview, but in practical terms we need to know a little more. When we send a request for a web page, let's say http://www.rooney.co.za for example, we send a GET request. This request is sent in normal text and could be read by any text editor.

The server responds and sends back a bunch of text data again. This will contain HTML tags that your browser can turn into an intelligent web page. If the web page was not found, you could get the "404 Not Found" error as a response. These status codes are usually on the first line of the response message.

Easy enough so far? Let's go over the basic architecture of the Servlet class.

The Servlet Architecture

Servlets are, as I've alluded to before, based on the applet architecture. If you're familiar with applets, you will see some distinct similarities. There are three methods that are important to us: init, service, and destroy:

- init: When a servlet is called by the server, it will run the init method. However, if there have been multiple requests for one particular servlet, the init method will not be re-invoked.

- service: The service method is where all the business of processing the HTTP request happens. This method can be re-invoked several times. We'll go into this in a lot more detail in the next section.

- destroy: When the server deems it necessary to clean up resources, the destroy method is called.

Servlets need to implement the javax.servlet.Servlet interface. To use this, you will have to download the latest version of the Servlets API from http://java.sun.com. You should look for the Java 5 version. This set of APIs needs to be installed, and your classpath must be updated.

Of course, if you have SAP Web Application Server 6.30 or later, you need not download J2EE. SAP has already provided the SAP J2EE for you.

Servlet Basics

The first thing we need to do if we want to code a servlet is decide how we are going to use it. We can implement the Servlet interface as mentioned before, or we can create a subclass of a class that already implements the interface (this is the option most people seem to use).

If we choose the latter option, again we have a choice. If we examine the APIs, we see that the GenericServlet class directly implements the Servlet interface, and we can use this directly or we can use one of *its* subclasses, namely HttpServlet.

If you're blessed with SAP NetWeaver Developer Studio, you will see the two choices in the drop-down menu for a new servlet, as shown in Figure 21-2. The methods available will change depending on the class you select.

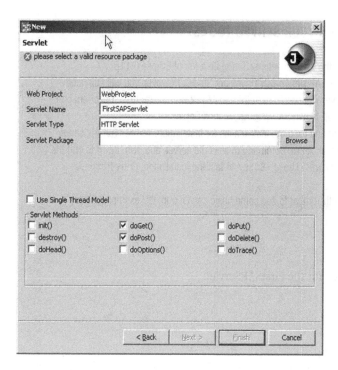

Figure 21-2. *The servlet builder from SAP NetWeaver Developer Studio*

Please don't worry if you don't have NetWeaver Developer Studio. This lesson will show you how to code servlets *without* using fancy tools.

The Generic Servlet

As I mentioned previously, the GenericServlet class is the first class we could choose to extend. So let's code up a very simple example of a servlet that is a direct subclass of the GenericServlet class. This will really just be an equivalent of the good old "Hello World" type of program that everyone starts off with.

Not all of us have access to expensive web and servlet servers, though. Fortunately, the fine people who make up the Apache open source consortium have written a very able web and servlet server called Tomcat. It's free to download, and we can use it to test our applications. In this way, we can set up a server on the same machine that we use to develop our application. This is good, because it enables us to *unit test* our application without disturbing the Basis people. See the sidebar entitled "Choosing Your Server to Test" for more details.

CHOOSING YOUR SERVER TO TEST

There are many different tools available to the J2EE developer. I'm quite a fan of Eclipse (http://www.eclipse.org), which is the basis for SAP NetWeaver Developer Studio. However, you will still need some sort of servlet engine and a web server. Apache Tomcat (http://jakarta.apache.org) offers both and saves you the need for testing with a full-blown SAP Web Application Server.

Download the latest version of Tomcat and read the instructions for installation. You can run the server as a Windows service, or you can issue the startup command to start the server, and shutdown to end the service. Point your web browser to http://localhost:8080/ to test the installation (or try http://127.0.0.1:8080/ if that doesn't work).

Go through the examples provided with Tomcat to see some basic servlet and JSP examples. These include code to make life easy!

Let's have a quick look at our code for the FirstSAPServlet:

```java
package servletPack;
import java.io.*;

import javax.servlet.GenericServlet;
import javax.servlet.ServletException;
import javax.servlet.ServletRequest;
import javax.servlet.ServletResponse;

public class FirstSAPServlet extends GenericServlet
{
   public void service(ServletRequest req, ServletResponse res)
     throws ServletException, IOException
   {
     res.setContentType("text/html");
     PrintWriter out = res.getWriter();

     out.println("<HTML>");
     out.println("<HEAD>");
     out.println("<TITLE>My First SAP Servlet</TITLE>");
     out.println("</HEAD>");
     out.println("<BODY>");
     out.println("<CENTER><H1>Hi ABAPers - Welcome to the future!</H1></CENTER>");
     out.println("</BODY>");
     out.println("</HTML>");


     out.close();
   }

}
```

As you can see in the preceding code, we are only overriding the service method. The other two methods will default to the superclass.

As I mentioned in the "Hypertext Transfer Protocol" section, there are two *flows* in a servlet. The *request* and the *response*. We have used the response stream in our program so that it "prints out" some HTML.

To make sure the response is treated as HTML, we must use the setContentType method from the ServletResponse class. Here we have specified "text/html" since we are using HTML in our response stream.

If you know any HTML, you will find it very easy to see what is happening here—HTML is tag-based and very similar to DIAG (SAP's screen protocol) in many ways. In the middle of the out.println lines, we are placing some text on the page: "Hi ABAPers – Welcome to the future!" This is centered and displayed as a heading (large and bold). This will then be interpreted by the browser, and we'll see the correct text displayed as a web page.

Before we compile this and test it, we should explore the mechanics behind the Servlet in general. Figure 21-3 clearly shows the three-tier structure. The request goes to the servlet engine; the servlet engine runs the Java class file and generates the response; and the response is interpreted by the client's browser, and the web page is displayed. Additionally, we could have extracted data or updated data in a database, though our example doesn't do that.

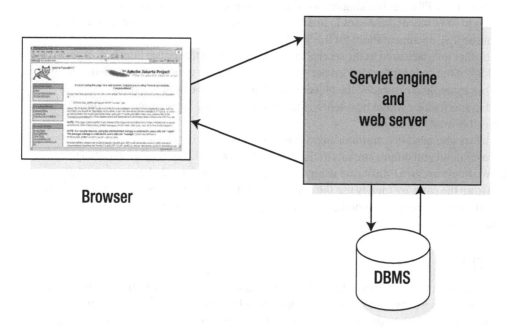

Figure 21-3. *Three-tier structure: browser, servlet engine, and DBMS*

There are some important directories in a web and servlet server that contain our Servlet classes. Most servers are configurable, so you should be able to point your servlet engine to the directory you would like to use.

The default in Tomcat is here:

```
<Tomcat Directory>\webapps\ROOT\WEB-INF\classes\
```

If you have a package structure, it must be in this directory. In other words, if you had a package named com.rooney.sapcon, your class files would be in this directory:

```
<Tomcat Directory>\webapps\ROOT\WEB-INF\classes\com\rooney\sapcon\
```

Remember that other class files can live in your directory. If your servlet needed other classes (and if you've done proper OO design, this should be the case) you would also have them in this directory.

This high-level overview is very entertaining, I hear you say, but it's not helping me run my "Hello World". To run a Servlet class file in the root directory, start your web server (Tomcat, in our case) and point your web browser to http://localhost:8080/servlet/FirstSAPServlet. You should see the "Hi ABAPers" message. Our first servlet is running!

Let's now take a more detailed look at the two interfaces we used in the service method. The first was the request interface, ServletRequest. Every time the method is called, the ServletRequest object is passed as an argument. There's a variety of information passed in this object, and by using some of the methods we can find out about the requesting client, the type of encoding used, the locale, and the content type. We can even interrogate any parameters that were passed as part of the request.

In the example, we didn't really make any use of the incoming request, but I hope you can see how we could. I'll cover tracking (cookies) in the "Tracking with Servlets" section later in the lesson to show one of these uses in practice. Please examine the API documentation (the J2EE not the J2SE documentation) for the ServletRequest.

The other interface used in the service method is the ServletResponse interface. If you have a look at the code for the FirstSAPServlet, you'll see that we've made extensive use of this one. In our example, we assigned the object to a reference res. We used the setContentType method to specify the content type sent to the client. In this case we set it for "text/html" and normally this would be the case.

What we also need to communicate with the client is an *output stream*. I purposefully didn't cover input and output streams in the first part of the book, but they're very straightforward. We simply assign a PrintWriter using the getWriter method. I called ours out, and as you can see from the code, we merely use the println method to send the text to the client. Again, this interface boasts several methods, which I strongly encourage you to research in the API documentation.

The HTTPServlet

This class, as you may have guessed, is tailored specifically for HTTP. The GenericServlet class will handle this, as we saw, but the HTTPServlet class will make life a little easier. Remember that this class extends the GenericServlet class and obeys all the normal inheritance rules. It lives in the javax.servlet.http package, so please ensure you have this import in your code.

The service method is broken down further into the following methods:

- doDelete(HttpServletRequest req, HttpServletResponse res): This method handles an HTTP DELETE request.

- doGet(HttpServletRequest req, HttpServletResponse res): This is certainly one of the most important methods. It handles the ubiquitous GET request.

- doOptions(HttpServletRequest req, HttpServletResponse res): This method allows the servlet to handle an OPTIONS request.

- doPost(HttpServletRequest req, HttpServletResponse res): This method allows the servlet to handle another common request, the POST.

- doPut(HttpServletRequest req, HttpServletResponse res): This method handles the—you guessed it—PUT request.

- doTrace(HttpServletRequest req, HttpServletResponse res): This method handles the TRACE request.

There are also a few other methods, which you should read up on.

In this section's example, we are going to put together a very simple Pet Shop system where we can order pets online and get a response to confirm what we have ordered. Feel free to expand on this example to make it more functional.

We will take the methods outlined above and add our own functionality to make them perform the actions we require. I'm going to concentrate on the GET and POST requests because these are the most common.

First, though, here's some HTML that displays a simple form in the browser:

```
<HTML>
<HEAD>
<TITLE>SAP Pet Shop</TITLE>
</HEAD>
<BODY>
<FORM METHOD = "POST"
      ACTION = "http://localhost:8080/Alistair/servlet/PetShop">

<PRE>
    *First Name: <INPUT TYPE = "text" NAME = "FNAME" >
    *Last Name: <INPUT TYPE = "text" NAME = "LNAME" >
          Email: <INPUT TYPE = "text" NAME = "EMAIL" >
</PRE>
<INPUT TYPE = "radio" NAME = "PET" VALUE = "cat">Cat<BR>
<INPUT TYPE = "radio" NAME = "PET" VALUE = "rat">Rat<BR>
<INPUT TYPE = "radio" NAME = "PET" VALUE = "dog">Dog<BR>
<INPUT TYPE = "radio" NAME = "PET" VALUE = "mole">Mole<BR>
<INPUT TYPE = "submit" VALUE = "submit Pet choice">
</FORM>
</BODY>
</HTML>
```

You can quite easily see from the preceding code and Figure 21-4 what is going on. I've put the most important parts in bold. The URL is the location of the servlet.

Tip If you're not familiar with HTML, don't worry. Put down this book and find a quick tutorial on the Net. It's not difficult to pick up the basics.

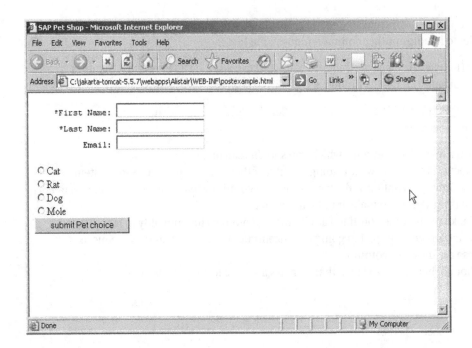

Figure 21-4. *The Pet Shop web page*

In the service method of our ChoosePet servlet, we will be able to gather information sent in the HttpServletRequest interface. For example, if I needed to see the selection of PET, I would do the following:

```
// Code snippet to show HttpServletRequest
String pet = request.getParameter("PET");
```

See how easy this is?

The response interface, HttpServletResponse, is a little different from ServletResponse. Essentially, though, we still have the same methods. We can set the content type using setContentType, and we can use getWriter to assign an output stream, just as we did with ServletResponse.

There are a bunch of other methods, which you will see in the documentation, including setStatus to send a status (like 404 Not Found) back to the browser. This is good for doing authorization checks.

Now we need to code our servlet. When the submit button is clicked, the HTML should send a POST request to a servlet called PetShop.java. Here's the code for this class:

```
import javax.servlet.http.*;
import java.io.*;
import javax.servlet.*;
/*
 * Created on 20-Jun-2005
 *
 */
```

```
/**
 * @author Alistair
 *
 * All rights reserved by Alistair Rooney (c) 2005
 * Unless specifically waived under Open Source Agreement
 *
 * 20-Jun-2005
 */
public class PetShop extends HttpServlet
{
    public void doPost(HttpServletRequest request, HttpServletResponse response)
     throws IOException, ServletException
     {
         response.setContentType("text/html");
         PrintWriter out = response.getWriter();
         out.println("<html>");
         out.println("<head>");
         out.println("<title>SAP Pet Shop</title>");
         out.println("</head>");
         out.println("<body>");
         out.println("<h1>Your Order has been Processed</h1><br><br>");
         out.println("Welcome "+ request.getParameter("FNAME")+ "<br>");
         out.println("You have chosen a "+ request.getParameter("PET"));
         out.println("</body>");
         out.println("</html>");
     }

    public void doGet(HttpServletRequest request, HttpServletResponse response)
     throws IOException, ServletException
     {
       this.doPost(request, response);
     }
}
```

The first thing you'll notice here is that the coding is remarkably similar to the coding in the GenericServlet (FirstSAPServlet), and it's quite simple. Notice, however, that I'm using the doPost method. If I didn't, I would probably get a 405 error message.

We can now enter information into our form and invoke our servlet. For now, I suggest putting your classes into the root directory. This saves us fiddling with a special file called web.xml—more on this file later.

You can call your HTML file directly from the browser, as shown in Figure 21-5. Enter your information, click the submit button, and viola! The servlet interprets the request and sends the response stream back to the browser, as shown in Figure 21-6.

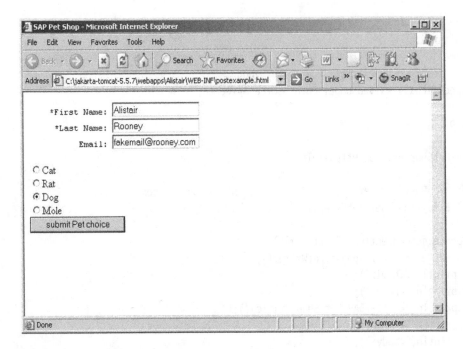

Figure 21-5. *Entering a Pet Shop order*

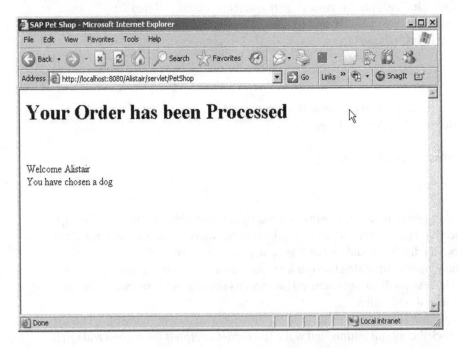

Figure 21-6. *The processed order*

Congratulations! You have completed your first J2EE application. The next step is to delve deeper into the technology behind servlets so that we can have better control over our applications.

The web.xml File

If you were observant when you were trying out your servlet, you will have noticed the web.xml file in the WEB-INF directory. Although we ignored it in the previous section, you can't ignore it in real life. This file carries the configuration of the servlet engine.

To be able to edit this file, you must have a very basic understanding of XML. If you don't, skip quickly ahead to the first section of Lesson 23. There's nothing scary about XML, it's really very simple.

To run the Pet Shop application in a directory other than the root directory, you have to "advertise" the presence of the servlet. There are two things that you must do before a servlet is recognized by Tomcat: declare the servlet's name and its location. The XML code that you need is here:

```
<?xml version="1.0" encoding="ISO-8859-1"?>
<!--
  Copyright 2004 The Apache Software Foundation

  Licensed under the Apache License, Version 2.0 (the "License");
  you may not use this file except in compliance with the License.
  You may obtain a copy of the License at

      http://www.apache.org/licenses/LICENSE-2.0

  Unless required by applicable law or agreed to in writing, software
  distributed under the License is distributed on an "AS IS" BASIS,
  WITHOUT WARRANTIES OR CONDITIONS OF ANY KIND, either express or implied.
  See the License for the specific language governing permissions and
  limitations under the License.
-->

<!DOCTYPE web-app
    PUBLIC "-//Sun Microsystems, Inc.//DTD Web Application 2.3//EN"
    "http://java.sun.com/dtd/web-app_2_3.dtd">

<web-app>


    <servlet>
        <servlet-name>PetShop</servlet-name>
        <servlet-class>PetShop</servlet-class>
    </servlet>
    <servlet-mapping>
        <servlet-name>PetShop</servlet-name>
        <url-pattern>/servlet/PetShop</url-pattern>
    </servlet-mapping>
    <servlet>
        <servlet-name>SAPServlet</servlet-name>
        <servlet-class>SAPServlet</servlet-class>
```

```
    </servlet>
    <servlet-mapping>
        <servlet-name>SAPServlet</servlet-name>
        <url-pattern>/servlet/SAPServlet</url-pattern>
    </servlet-mapping>
```

```
</web-app>
```

As you have probably noticed, I have two servlets in this XML. One called PetShop, which you know all about, and the other is called SAPServlet, which you needn't be concerned with since it points to another servlet not covered here.

The servlet declaration sets the name used to refer to the class, and the servlet-mapping declaration identifies its location. If I had chosen to use an arbitrary name for the servlet, like FrogHopper for instance, I could have put the following into my XML file:

```
<servlet>
    <servlet-name>FrogHopper</servlet-name>
    <servlet-class>PetShop</servlet-class>
</servlet>
<servlet-mapping>
    <servlet-name>FrogHopper</servlet-name>
    <url-pattern>/servlet/PetShop</url-pattern>
</servlet-mapping>
```

Notice that I have not changed the name of the class, but I have changed the name I use to refer to it. Of course, you would have to make one more important change before this would work. In our original HTML form, we would need to change the action to read the name of the reference FrogHopper:

```
<FORM METHOD = "POST"
      ACTION = "http://localhost:8080/Alistair/servlet/FrogHopper">
```

That's not all we can do with these tags. We can point to a class within a package deep in the directory structure. So we could have this:

```
<servlet>
    <servlet-name>FrogHopper</servlet-name>
    <servlet-class>com.sap.demos.PetShop</servlet-class>
</servlet>
```

I've included the servlet mapping tag for completeness. This will assign a URL to your servlet.

Initializing Servlets

Most programmers tend to avoid hard-coded values because they remove flexibility and create maintenance overhead. However, it would be slightly remiss of me not to discuss initialization parameters in this section on the web.xml configuration file. It is possible to pass initialization parameters into our servlet.

Let's change our Pet Shop servlet to accept startup parameters that have been hard-coded into our XML file. (These parameters can be generated by other means, so they will not always be hard-coded.) The first thing we need is an init method. Here's the code, with the new parts in bold:

```java
import javax.servlet.http.*;
import java.io.*;
import javax.servlet.*;
/*
 * Created on 20-Jun-2005
 *
 */


/**
 * @author Alistair
 *
 * All rights reserved by Alistair Rooney (c) 2005
 * Unless specifically waived under Open Source Agreement
 *
 * 20-Jun-2005
 */
public class PetShop extends HttpServlet
{
private String pageTitle;

    public void init(ServletConfig config) throws ServletException
    {
        super.init(config);
        pageTitle = config.getInitParameter("pageTitle");
    }
    public void doPost(HttpServletRequest request, HttpServletResponse response)
    throws IOException, ServletException
    {
    response.setContentType("text/html");
    PrintWriter out = response.getWriter();
    out.println("<html>");
    out.println("<head>");
    out.println("<title>"+pageTitle+"</title>");
    out.println("</head>");
    out.println("<body>");
    out.println("<h1>Your Order has been Processed</h1><br><br>");
    out.println("Welcome "+ request.getParameter("FNAME")+ "<br>");
    out.println("You have chosen a "+ request.getParameter("PET"));
    out.println("</body>");
    out.println("</html>");
    }


}
```

Lovely! I've changed the code to allow for parameters to be passed from the config file (web.xml). Now we need to alter my web.xml file to include my hard-coded parameters. We do this by using a new tag, the init-param tag. Here's the changed file:

```xml
<?xml version="1.0" encoding="ISO-8859-1"?>
<!--
  Copyright 2004 The Apache Software Foundation

  Licensed under the Apache License, Version 2.0 (the "License");
  you may not use this file except in compliance with the License.
  You may obtain a copy of the License at

      http://www.apache.org/licenses/LICENSE-2.0

  Unless required by applicable law or agreed to in writing, software
  distributed under the License is distributed on an "AS IS" BASIS,
  WITHOUT WARRANTIES OR CONDITIONS OF ANY KIND, either express or implied.
  See the License for the specific language governing permissions and
  limitations under the License.
-->

<!DOCTYPE web-app
    PUBLIC "-//Sun Microsystems, Inc.//DTD Web Application 2.3//EN"
    "http://java.sun.com/dtd/web-app_2_3.dtd">

<web-app>

    <servlet>
        <servlet-name>PetShop</servlet-name>
        <servlet-class>PetShop</servlet-class>
        <init-param>
            <param-name>pageTitle</param-name>
            <param-title>My new Servlet Title!</param-title>
        </init-param>
    </servlet>
    <servlet-mapping>
        <servlet-name>PetShop</servlet-name>
        <url-pattern>/servlet/PetShop</url-pattern>
    </servlet-mapping>
    <servlet>
        <servlet-name>SAPServlet</servlet-name>
        <servlet-class>SAPServlet</servlet-class>
    </servlet>
    <servlet-mapping>
        <servlet-name>SAPServlet</servlet-name>
        <url-pattern>/servlet/SAPServlet</url-pattern>
    </servlet-mapping>

</web-app>
```

We should now have everything we need to try out our new servlet. We'll run it exactly as we did before. The result is shown in Figure 21-7. Notice the title of the web page!

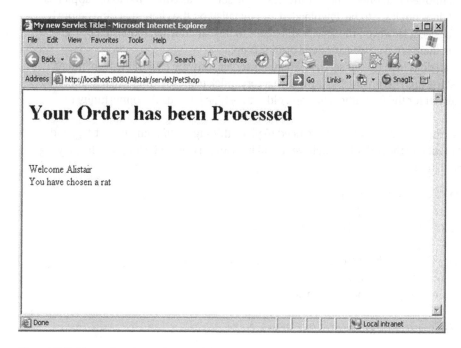

Figure 21-7. *Changing the web page title*

Global Initialization Parameters

What if you had parameters that were global in nature? In other words, you had a value that you wanted all the servlets in a specific directory (Web-App) to use as a parameter. We achieve this by using the context-param tag.

Note When using the context-param tag, you will only be able to access the value of the parameter from the ServletContext object and not from the ServletConfig object that we saw in the previous example.

```
<web-app>
    <context-param>
      <param-name>contextParm</param-name>
      <param-value>Java Rules!</param-value>
    </context-param>
</web-app>
```

This snippet of XML shows how you can use the context-param tag. Again, I need to point out that hard-coding values in this way undermines good programming practice.

Preloading Servlets

Previously I mentioned that one of the advantages of the servlet, as compared to the applet, is that the servlet does not have to be downloaded and installed on the client machine before it is available to be used. However, the servlet still needs to be loaded when requested by the client. However, there is a way we can speed even this up!

What we can do is load up our servlets when our server software (SAP J2EE, WebSphere, Tomcat, etc.) starts up. This ensures that we have a very quick response time when the client requests the servlet for the first time. The good old web.xml file gives us the opportunity to configure this.

The tag we use is load-on-startup. We need to place this tag *within* our servlet tag, and we also need to specify the order in which we would like our servlets to be loaded. The new tag is shown in bold in the following code:

```
<?xml version="1.0" encoding="ISO-8859-1"?>
<!--
 Copyright 2004 The Apache Software Foundation

 Licensed under the Apache License, Version 2.0 (the "License");
 you may not use this file except in compliance with the License.
 You may obtain a copy of the License at

     http://www.apache.org/licenses/LICENSE-2.0

 Unless required by applicable law or agreed to in writing, software
 distributed under the License is distributed on an "AS IS" BASIS,
 WITHOUT WARRANTIES OR CONDITIONS OF ANY KIND, either express or implied.
 See the License for the specific language governing permissions and
 limitations under the License.
-->

<!DOCTYPE web-app
    PUBLIC "-//Sun Microsystems, Inc.//DTD Web Application 2.3//EN"
    "http://java.sun.com/dtd/web-app_2_3.dtd">

<web-app>

<servlet>
        <servlet-name>PetShop</servlet-name>
        <servlet-class>PetShop</servlet-class>
        <init-param>
            <param-name>pageTitle</param-name>
            <param-title>My new Servlet Title!</param-title>
        </init-param>
        <load-on-startup>1</load-on-startup>
```

```
    </servlet>
      <servlet-mapping>
        <servlet-name>PetShop</servlet-name>
        <url-pattern>/servlet/PetShop</url-pattern>
    </servlet-mapping>
    <servlet>
        <servlet-name>SAPServlet</servlet-name>
        <servlet-class>SAPServlet</servlet-class>
    </servlet>
    <servlet-mapping>
        <servlet-name>SAPServlet</servlet-name>
        <url-pattern>/servlet/SAPServlet</url-pattern>
    </servlet-mapping>

</web-app>
```

There are many more deployment descriptor tags available for the web.xml file. If you are interested in them in a general sense, BEA Systems has a list of the most popular ones and their use (http://e-docs.bea.com/wls/docs61/webapp/web_xml.html). You need to be aware, though, that this is for the BEA WebLogic server, and some tags might not work on other servers.

If you are using NetWeaver Developer Studio you will find that your XML will be built for you depending on your entries in the pages you select. You will see a node named web.xml.

Note In the SAP WAS 6.40 we now use web-j2ee-engine.xml to store some of the tags and not web.xml. It can be confusing!

Servlet Timeout

Before we leave the web.xml file, let's examine another useful configuration tag. The timeout value for a servlet is the time that it will stay loaded in memory. If it unloads too quickly, the next client to use it will have to wait again while it loads up. This may be good or bad, depending on your application, number of clients, and other variables.

The following code snippet shows that we have overridden the default timeout. (The default depends on your server, but it's normally 30 minutes.) In this example, we are specifying 25 minutes:

```
<web-app>
    <session-config>
        <session-timeout>25</session-timeout>
    </session-config>
</web-app>
```

Tracking with Servlets

There is always a fine line between privacy and convenience. I'm fairly sure that few people would like the slightly dystopian world in the film *Minority Report*, where passers-by were scanned by machines, and tailored advertisements were then displayed on the digital billboards as they passed.

On the other hand, many people like the clever way that some web sites automatically recognize their presence and sign them on automatically if they use the same computer. Some, like Amazon.com, even give the client a list of recommended reading based on previous purchases or on the books displayed. There are many other useful ways that tracking can work for us, and modern browsers allow us to switch off tracking if we have privacy concerns.

There are a few ways that tracking can be achieved. SSL is one, URL rewriting is another, but we will concentrate on cookies. Coding cookies into our programs is wonderfully easy!

Programming Cookies

Cookies work with keys, and the values that belong to those keys. This arrangement is known as key/value pairs.

Remember our request and response model? We made use of the HttpServletRequest and HttpServletResponse objects. If you go through the API documentation for these objects, you will come across some cookie methods. In HttpServletResponse you will find the addCookie method, and in the HttpServletRequest class you will find the getCookie method. Yes! It's that easy.

Cookies can then be read and be used for many different purposes. For example, they may grant you access to a site that you would otherwise have to register for, they could bring up a custom page based on your prior activity (like Amazon.com), or they can retain certain session data for your convenience.

In the next lesson, we will extend our servlet knowledge into JavaServer Pages.

■ ■ ■

JavaServer Pages (JSP)

JSP pages are a natural extension of servlets. With JSP, you can code your entire program within an HTML page. If you haven't learned the basics of HTML, do it now. If you already know enough HTML to get by, sit back and enjoy our journey into JSP.

The basic principle behind JSP is very simple. In fact, coding your first JSP page will take less than 5 minutes! However, JSP can be a very complex area as we can merge two technologies (HTML and Java) quite successfully.

A JSP page is, quite simply, an HTML file with special tags that allow us to embed Java code directly into the HTML source code. The server then takes this JSP code and translates it into a servlet, which is then run as a normal servlet.

BUSINESS SERVER PAGES

Business Server Pages (BSP) is part of the SAP WAS environment. BSP pages act much like JSP pages save for one very notable difference. They use ABAP code instead of Java.

Here's an example of a BSP page that produces five "Hello Worlds" increasing in size each time. Can you see the ABAP code here?

```
<%@page language="abap"%>
<html>
<body>
<center>
<% do 5 times. %>
  <font size="<%= sy-index %>">
  Hello World<br>
  </font>
<% enddo.  %>
</center>
</body>
<html>
```

This is very cool. Of course JSP pages will run on any server, including SAP J2EE.
Once we have covered JSP, come back and review this code and note the similarities.

The JSP Architecture

When we looked at servlets, we saw that the servlet engine and a web server act together to produce a result on the client. With a JSP page, we need another tool called a JSP server! This will read the JSP files and produce a servlet source and class. This servlet is then run in the normal way.

Let's take a quick look at the sequence of events:

1. A request is sent to the web server, which then passes it to the JSP server.

2. The JSP server locates the JSP file requested.

3. The JSP server checks the version of the JSP page to see if it has used it before.

4. If it has not, it will create a new servlet and compile it into a class.

5. Control is passed to the servlet engine, which runs the servlet.

6. The generated response is sent to the client (usually a browser).

Most servers (such as BEA WebLogic, SAP WAS, IBM WebSphere, and Sun Application Server) will already have a JSP engine as an integral part of the architecture. We will be using Apache Tomcat again, since it is freely available.

The JSP Access Model

Most companies (SAP included) agree that the Model-View-Controller (MVC) pattern is the best way to implement JSP. The MVC basically tries to separate the business logic from the presentation logic, resulting in a more robust and scalable application. It does this by separating the logic into three separate and distinct areas: the Model, the View, and—you guessed it—the Controller.

In our JSP environment, this translates to the Model being JavaBeans, the View being the JSP, and the Controller being the generated servlet. Figure 22-1 illustrates this schematically.

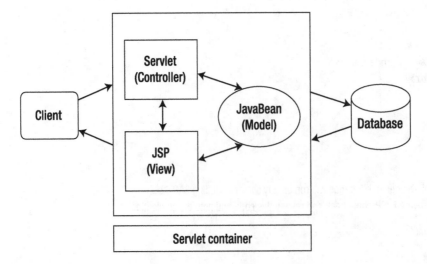

Figure 22-1. *The MVC model*

Much has been written about the MVC model, both within SAP and in a more general sense. Adding to that wealth of information would be redundant, so, again, I encourage you to research this further.

The JSP Syntax

JSP 2.0 has introduced some very useful new elements. Some of these are the *Expression Language, tag handlers,* and the new *JSP XML syntax.* We will examine some of these at the end of the lesson, but first let's examine the basics.

- Scripting elements

- Directives

- Action elements

Scripting Elements

Scripting elements have the following syntax:

```
<% %>
```

They can be categorized into the following categories:

- Comments

- Expressions

- Scriptlets

- Declarations

We've actually already had a glimpse of comments in the BSP sidebar. As you might imagine, these are fairly simple.

Comments

Comments always take this form:

```
<%-- --%>
```

Comments merely tell the developer more about the code. They are ignored by the servlet generator. Don't get confused by these and HTML comments—we will explore a major difference between them later in the lesson.

Here's an example of a comment:

```
<%-- Change requested by FI team to display GL account - 24th August 2005  --%>
```

Easy enough, I think you'll agree.

Expressions

Expressions take this form:

```
<%=    %>
```

Expressions convert a Java statement directly into a string for the servlet to output. The string would normally be a return value from a getter or accessor method. Typically this method lives in a JavaBeans class. I'll cover JavaBeans in the "JavaBean Elements" section later in this lesson.

Have a look at a small example:

```
<%= CustomerBean.getName() %>
```

Note that there is no semicolon after the expression.

Let's have a look at an example program that uses an expression:

```
<html>
<head>
<title>My First JSP File</title>
</head>
<body>
<!-- This is an example of an HTML comment -->
<font color="#996699"><h1 align="center">My First JSP Page</h1></font>
<h3 align="center"><font color="#996600">
   Apache Server reports the time and date is:</font>
<%-- This is an example of a JSP comment --%>
<font color="#993333"><%=new java.util.Date() %></font></h3>
</body>
</html>
```

Save this with the .jsp extension (for example, FirstJSP.jsp). All you have to do now is make sure that your chosen web application server is running and point your browser to the correct file.

Look at Figure 22-2. It shows that I have stored the file in the directory shown in Figure 22-3. Notice that the address in the browser is http://localhost:8080/Alistair/FirstJSP.jsp. The server automatically routes me to <Tomcat-Home>/webapps/Alistair and looks for the JSP file there.

Easy, isn't it! Let's recap what we have done and what the system has done. We created a normal HTML file (in the editor of your choice—SAP advises Eclipse or NetWeaver Developer Studio, but you could use Notepad). After that, we started the server (Tomcat in the example) and pointed a browser to the JSP file. This pulled the JSP file into the Tomcat JSP engine. It generated a servlet and passed it to the normal web server to run it. We then saw the end result.

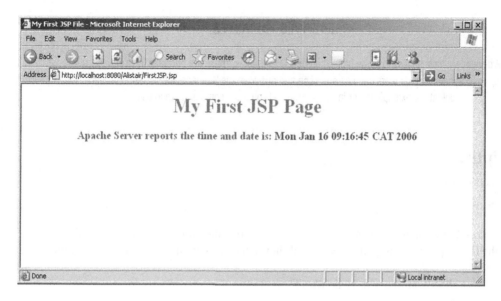

Figure 22-2. *My very first JSP page*

Figure 22-3. *The directory structure*

From JSP 1.2 onwards, we can use XML to define our tags. XML is case-sensitive, and we should take care *not* to mix XML tags and the old format tags. The expression tag in XML is as follows:

```
<jsp:expression> CustomerBean.getName() </jsp:expression>
```

JSP 2.0 now includes Expression Language, which contains the following advanced features:

- Basic arithmetic

- Basic comparisons

- Implicit objects

- Functions

These are very simple to use and well worth exploring further.

Scriptlets

Scriptlets take this form:

```
<%  %>
```

Scriptlets are where JSP gets very powerful. You can embed full sections of Java code right into the HTML page. Not only that, but, as I'll show later, you can mix and match HTML and Java code!

Here's a short example of a "Hello World" program:

```
<% String myString = request.getParameter("passString");
      out.println(myString);
%>
```

In this example, I would have passed "Hello World" as my parameter passString.

Of course, there is an XML version of the preceding expression. Have a look at the following example and see if you can figure out what's going on.

```
<jsp:scriptlet> for (int j=0; j<4; j++)
                     { </jsp:scriptlet>
<H<jsp:expression>j</jsp:expression>>Hi
ABAPers</H<jsp:expression>j</jsp:expression>>
<jsp:scriptlet>}</jsp:scriptlet>
```

If your HTML is not very good, don't worry. SAP provides a Tag Library for you to browse. H*n* simply tells HTML to print a heading line of size *n*, where 1 is the largest. Code this up and see what it produces.

Declarations

Declarations take this form:

```
<%!  %>
```

And the XML format is as follows (remember XML is case-sensitive):

```
<jsp:declaration></jsp:declaration>
```

Declarations are used for just that—declaring stuff. We can declare variables like so:

```
<%! int counter = 0; %>
```

We can also declare entire methods as shown here:

```
<%! public double calcArea(double radius)
    {
        return Math.PI * radius * radius;
    }
%>
```

Conventional wisdom dictates that we do not overload our HTML with scriptlets. The way around this for complex tasks (or for database interaction) is to use JavaBeans (which will be discussed in the "JavaBean Elements" section later in this lesson).

Directives

Directives take this format:

```
<%@ %>
```

A directive allows the JSP developer to take control over many of the configuration aspects of the JSP page. We've seen one of these directives already in the sidebar on Business Server Pages. We declared the language we used in a page directive at the top of the BSP page. In that case, the language was ABAP. Of course, in JSP development we will be specifying the language as Java. This isn't always strictly necessary, but there are a number of other attributes of the page directive that are far more useful.

We can even do Java imports using the page directive:

```
<%@ page import = "java.util.*, com.sap.jco.*" %>
```

Here are some of the common directives that are used:

- autoflush
- buffer
- contentType
- errorpage
- extends
- import
- info
- isErrorPage
- isThreadSafe
- language
- pageEncoding
- session

We won't be going into each of these, but there are one or two that are very smart. The contentType directive is very useful. It can be used to do smart things like embed Excel into your JSP page. We would do this with the following directive:

```
<%@ page contentType="application/vnd.ms-excel" %>
```

We can even do this dynamically, without using a directive, by using one of the methods provided in the response object. Let's see that in code:

```
response.setContentType("application/vnd.ms-excel");
```

This way we could have normal HTML *and* Excel on the same JSP page. Cool, is it not?

We can also make our JSP page an error page so that we can give the user a meaningful explanation when things don't go quite right. We do this by using isErrorPage:

```
<%@ page isErrorPage="true" %>
```

That ends our discussion of directives, but I should mention the XML equivalent of the include directive. The XML include behaves exactly like an ABAP include:

```
<jsp:directive.include file="a file to include" />
```

If you're a little confused about the XML syntax here, look ahead to Lesson 23 on XML.

Action Elements

Action elements are more runtime oriented than the other tags. They can be broken down into three distinct categories:

- Control elements
- JavaBean elements
- Custom tags

Control Elements

Control elements allow control to be passed to another JSP file or even to the Java plug-in that is part of the browser. Let's examine some of these tags. The syntax is XML based, so if you're not yet comfortable with XML, skip ahead to Lesson 23 (on XML) first and then return here.

The first tag, plugin, allows you to run an applet in a browser. This tag is likely to see less use as time goes on—applets are not as fashionable as they once were, and Microsoft and Sun are now friends again, so it's reasonable to expect that future browsers will fully support Java, thus doing away with the need for plug-ins.

The syntax for this tag is as follows:

```
<jsp:plugin type="applet" code="myClass.class" width="200" height="300" >
</jsp:plugin>
```

As you can see, this tag permits control over most of the attributes you normally would control from an HTML page.

The second control element I'd like to introduce is `fallback`. Whenever we have a situation where the client may not support a piece of code in our JSP page, we want to fall back to a default message. This is like when you try to load a movie clip in your web browser and you get a message asking you to download and install some additional software.

Let's combine `fallback` with `plugin` to get a picture of where we would use it:

```
<jsp:plugin type="applet" code="myClass.class" width="200" height="300" >
    <jsp:fallback>You have not installed the Java plug-in</jsp:fallback>
</jsp:plugin>
```

It's important to take note of the nesting here. The `fallback` tag is nested inside the `plugin` tag.

The next control element tag to look at is the `params` tag, which is used primarily for passing parameters to the next JSP page or applet. In order to illustrate this, let's expand on the previous example:

```
<jsp:plugin type="applet" code="myClass.class" width="200" height="300" >
    <jsp:params>
      <jsp:param name="radius" value="7.43" />
      <jsp:param name="circum" value="23.7" />
    </jsp:params>
    <jsp:fallback>You have not installed the Java plug-in</jsp:fallback>
</jsp:plugin>
```

As you can see, there are actually two tags here. The first specifies that we will be using parameters, and the second (`param`—notice the absence of an "s" at the end) details the parameter names and their values.

The final control element I'd like to cover is the `forward` tag. This is very similar to the `include` tag. The big difference is that control is now passed to the new JSP file and not returned to the calling JSP page. Of course, we could use this in conjunction with our parameters to make a call that is very similar in many ways to an ABAP `PERFORM` statement. Here's a trivial example:

```
<jsp:forward page="newJSP.jsp">
    <jsp:params>
      <jsp:param name="radius" value="7.43" />
      <jsp:param name="circum" value="23.7" />
    </jsp:params>
</jsp:forward>
```

Easy enough, I think you'll agree. If you don't agree, please write your complaint on the back of a $100 bill, and post it to me.

JavaBean Elements

Please cast your eyes back to the Model-View-Controller (MVC) diagram in Figure 22-1. As you can see, it shows our business logic separate from the other code. This has many advantages.

Separating out business logic is not new to ABAP programmers. We have been exposed to a three-tier structure in SAP for many years now. The main reason behind this was to ensure smooth scalability—we can increase our transaction servers and our presentation servers as the demand for IT evolves in an organization.

The MVC pattern not only allows us a large degree of scalability—it also separates our business logic from our presentation logic. This is a good thing, since it means we can implement changes to our business model without having an effect on our client.

We use the MVC pattern in JSP (and in many other areas) by making use of a JavaBean to run our business logic.

Before the days of IBM WebSphere, IBM brought out a development environment called VisualAge for Java. One of the features of this software was that you could produce a Java application without writing a single line of code! This was done by visually "plugging" JavaBeans together. All the developer needed to do was determine how and when each JavaBean was called.

JavaBeans are plug-in Java programs. Essentially they are ordinary Java classes, but they must adhere to a few rules:

- A JavaBean should always have a constructor with no arguments.

- There should be *no* public instance variables in a JavaBean. Of course, if you have been coding correctly, you should already be doing this.

- Instance variables must have getter and setter methods that are public.

Before we can make use of a JavaBean, we must identify it and obtain a reference to it. We do this by using <jsp:useBean> as in the following example:

```
<jsp:useBean id="circArea" class="area.CircleArea" scope="session"/>
```

You should see three attributes in the preceding example. The first one gives our class a reference name that we can use subsequently. The second links this to our actual class name (in the package area), and the third determines the scope. The first two are fairly self-explanatory, but I'd like to dwell on scope for a moment.

Scope is similar to plain old Java scope—its visibility to other programs. If you leave scope out, it will default to page, which means that the JSP page will only be visible to the first request. A value of request has the same effect as page, but if there are any jsp:include or jsp:forward tags, those JSP pages will also be visible to the request. If you use session, as in our example, the JSP page will be visible to all requests of the current client session. The last level is application, which makes the JSP page visible to all sessions in the WAS.

JSP syntax defines three tags to use with JavaBeans: useBean, setProperty, and getProperty. The setProperty and getProperty tags allow the developer to fetch and change the properties (variables) of the JavaBean. This is exactly like using a get or set method within a Java program. In fact, I could choose to use a scriptlet and do exactly that. Let's extend our previous example a little to include a setProperty tag:

```
<jsp:useBean id="circArea" class="area.CircleArea" scope="session"/>
<jsp:setProperty  name="circArea" property="setRadius" value="5.74"/>
```

I'm sure that you can make out what is happening in this code.

JAVA REFLECTION

Java has an amazing ability. It can expose its classes, methods, and attributes to us at runtime. This is termed *reflection*. If your HTML form uses the same variable names as your JavaBean, you can use the "*" symbol in your value and it will automatically set and get the correct values for you.

Reflection is an incredibly useful extension of Java, and it's well worth spending a little time researching it.

At this point in the lesson, I strongly encourage you to build a small test application using a JSP page and a JavaBean. You can model this on the Pet Shop application we looked at in Lesson 21, and perhaps expand it a little.

Custom Tags

The topic of custom tags has traditionally been a complex one. The benefit of using custom tags is that you can set up your own tags to perform sets of routines. In this way, they are very similar to ABAP macros. However, until recently using custom tags has been much more diffi-cult than setting up a simple macro.

With the advent of JSP 2.0, this has been made a lot easier. The secret is the new tag file. To write a tag file, you simply create a normal text file with tag elements inside it. The only ele-ment you cannot use is a directive.

Let's create a tag file called myFirstTag.tag, and fill it with the following code:

```
<%
 String abapers = "ABAP Programmers";
%>

Hello There,  <%= abapers %>
```

Save this file in a folder called tags in the WEB-INF directory.

You will now need to include the following line in your JSP page:

```
<%@ taglib prefix="tags" tagdir="/WEB-INF/tags" %>
```

Now all we need is to add our new tag where we need it in our JSP:

```
<tags:myFirstTag/>
```

This will now print out "Hello There, ABAP Programmers".

If you are familiar with the old way of using custom tags, you will be breathing a sigh of relief. This is a lot easier! However, there is a catch. To use this, you must have a JSP server that supports these new tag files, like Tomcat 5. At the time of writing, the latest WAS 6.40 does not support JSP 2.0, but I'm sure WAS 7.0 will.

This concludes our introduction to JSP development. Of course, there is an awful lot more to JSP development than can fit in this short lesson. I recommend that you do some further reading (and code up a few examples) on the following JSP-related subjects:

- Security

- Filters

- Using JSP and servlets together

Entire volumes have been written on JSP, so information will be easy to find!

In the next lesson, we will explore XML.

LESSON 23

■■■

Extensible Markup Language (XML)

It may surprise you to know that HTML and XML share a common heritage. They are both derived from Standardized General Markup Language (SGML). SGML, or ISO 8879, was developed to define document formats and how documents may be used.

HTML, of course, predated XML, and it is a very easy way to mark up web pages. Even if you have no HTML experience, you can be creating pretty complex web pages after a few hours! What HTML does not allow, though, is extensibility, validations, and structure, so XML was born.

XML is a meta-language. In other words, the language itself contains data to describe itself. It does this by using tags, as we have seen in previous lessons. The really neat thing about this is that you can describe your own tags. You are not limited, as you are with HTML, to predefined tags. This is the *extensible* aspect of XML. Because of this extensibility, a number of other languages have grown out of XML.

There are also some side projects that are derived from XML. In particular, Extensible Stylesheet Language for Transformations (XSLT). This allows you to transform XML documents into other document type formats. Since SAP is making use of this technology within the NetWeaver stack, I encourage you to read up on this.

XML must be *structured*. Even though we can add our own tags, they must have an order and a structure. We will see this later when we have a look at some examples.

XML is also self-validating. There are two aspects to this: the document must be *well-formed* and it must be *valid*. We will explore these two aspects in more detail.

Finally, these attributes make XML ideal for communicating between applications. That is why SAP uses it within Exchange Infrastructure.

The Sales Order Example

Let's concoct a trivial example of a sales order. I say trivial, because if you have explored the SAP Sales and Distribution module, you will know how complex a real sales order can be! Have a look at the following code and see if you can work out what data is being represented. It's easy really.

```
<?xml version="1.0" encoding="UTF-8" standalone="yes"?>
<!--The Sales Order example -->
<order number="5072341">
  <orderDate>20050801</orderDate>
  <soldTo>14432</soldTo>
  <shipTo>14476</shipTo>
  <delDate>20050815</delDate>
  <poNumber>90-6627-3</poNumber>
  <line id="010">
    <material>GI-72388</material>
    <uom>ea</uom>
    <unitPrice>765.00</unitPrice>
    <qty>35</qty>
  </line>
  <line id="020">
    <material>GI-34490</material>
    <uom>ea</uom>
    <unitPrice>200.00</unitPrice>
    <qty>76</qty>
  </line>
  <line id="030">
    <material>GI-982254</material>
    <uom>ea</uom>
    <unitPrice>25.00</unitPrice>
    <qty>12</qty>
  </line>
  <comment>Deliver at bay 3</comment>
</order>
```

Before we go any further, it's important to note that there are *standard* sales order formats that have been devised by Electronic Data Interchange (EDI) regulation agencies in different parts of the world.

So let us explore the preceding sales order. The first thing you should be able to see is that XML tags are paired. For each start tag, there is an end tag (though, there is a way around this rule that we will see later). If we look at the <order> start tag, we can see that there is a corresponding </order> end tag. Don't worry about the number for now; just note that the forward slash denotes the end tag. If you are familiar with HTML, you will have seen this before.

Note Please note that XML, like Java, is case-sensitive. "Order" is not the same as "order"!

When we examine the quantity tags, <qty>12</qty>, we can see that we have content. Collectively, this combination of opening tag, closing tag, and content is called the *element*. I think it is obvious that we are saying that this item has a quantity of 12 units.

Element names can be anything, but they should be descriptive so that we can read the XML code easily. We also have some extra rules to conform to:

- The name of an element must start with a letter or the underscore (_).

- An element may not start with the letters "XML" or "xml" or any other variation.

- The second character and any others can be periods, hyphens, underscores, colons, or letters.

- An element name may not contain spaces.

We can also see in our example that we can *nest* our elements. Just make sure that the nesting order is correct. You should be familiar with this from nested loops, if statements, and the like, from ABAP. For example, this is correct:

```
<address>
  <street>1234 Main Street</street>
</address>
```

This is clearly wrong:

```
<street><address>1234 Main Street</street></address>
```

Empty Elements

I said that all start tags must have end tags, but there is an exception to this. It's when we use an empty element. Instead of writing this:

```
<comment></comment>
```

we can abbreviate it by saying this:

```
<comment/>
```

Please be aware that an empty element does not mean that there is nothing at all in the tag. It just means that the element has no *content*.

Element Attributes

In the earlier sales order example, we saw that some elements had information *as part of the tag*. This is known as an *attribute*. It gives us information about the tag itself. Here's an example:

```
<order number="5072341">
```

This tells us that the order has a number attribute.

The data must be in quotes. You may use single or double quotes, but the convention seems to be to use double quotes. This keeps it in line with Java.

Note It is generally accepted that only internal information should be stored as an attribute. This means that data that is not generally presented to a client can be stored as an attribute. In our sales order example, therefore, it is not correct to represent the order number as an attribute. Can you think of a better attribute?

That's the general syntax of XML—I'm sure that you'll agree that it is fairly straightforward. If you were just looking for XML basics so you could understand the code in a previous lesson, feel free to go back again. In the next sections we will explore XML in more detail.

The Document Header

The document header consists of processing instructions, otherwise known as PI tags. These tags are identified with a question mark after the angle bracket:

```
<?   ?>
```

A common example of a processing instruction is the XML declaration. In the earlier sales order example, you will see one:

```
<?xml version="1.0" encoding="UTF-8" standalone="yes"?>
```

There are several attributes available for the document header, but this example shows three common ones. The first identifies the version, which in our case is version 1.0. The second attribute identifies the character set, and as you can see, we are not using Unicode here—we should always try to use Unicode. The third attribute tells the parser that this XML document does not require any other documents. We will cover external documents when we discuss *validating* the XML with schemas or the Document Type Definition (DTD).

We will encounter more PI tags as we progress.

The Document Content

Let's return to our sales order example. The note in the "Element Attributes" section pointed out a problem with the original code, so I've refined the example to make it a little more correct.

```
<?xml version="1.0" encoding="UTF-8" standalone="yes"?>
<!—The Sales Order example -->
<order type="ZQ">
  <number>5072341</number>
  <orderDate>20050801</orderDate>
  <soldTo>14432</soldTo>
  <shipTo>14476</shipTo>
  <delDate>20050815</delDate>
  <poNumber>90-6627-3</poNumber>
  <line id="010">
    <material>GI-72388</material>
    <uom>ea</uom>
    <unitPrice>765.00</unitPrice>
    <qty>35</qty>
  </line>
  <line id="020">
    <material>GI-34490</material>
    <uom>ea</uom>
```

```
    <unitPrice>200.00</unitPrice>
    <qty>76</qty>
  </line>
  <line id="030">
    <material>GI-982254</material>
    <uom>ea</uom>
    <unitPrice>25.00</unitPrice>
    <qty>12</qty>
  </line>
  <comment>Deliver at bay 3</comment>
</order>
```

The first thing that needs to be stressed is that there can be only one *root* tag. A root tag is the highest level tag in the document. In our document, you can see that the root tag is <order>. Attempting to have more than one root element will cause an error when trying to parse this document.

Now suppose we had a purchase order XML document that also had a comment tag, a unit tag, a qty tag, and so on? How could we differentiate between the sales order elements and the purchase order elements?

The way that this problem is solved in XML is to qualify the tags using *namespaces*. We identify the namespace we are going to use in the root element. Here's an example:

```
<arcXML:order xmlns:arcXML="http://www.rooney.co.za/arcXML">
```

In our root element, we now have an xmlns (XML namespace) tag pointing to a URL. We can prefix all our element names (as we have with the order) with the shorthand code arcXML. This effectively makes them unique, so that any other XML document that has similar tags will not result in a collision if we choose to use those tags in our document.

Let's revisit the sales order example again and put our new qualifier in front of the first few tags:

```
<arcXML:number>5072341</arcXML:number>
  <arcXML:orderDate>20050801</arcXML:orderDate>
  <arcXML:soldTo>14432</arcXML:soldTo>
  <arcXML:shipTo>14476</arcXML:shipTo>
  <arcXML:delDate>20050815</arcXML:delDate>
  <arcXML:poNumber>90-6627-3</arcXML:poNumber>
  <arcXML:line id="010">
    <arcXML:material>GI-72388</arcXML:material>
    <arcXML:uom>ea</arcXML:uom>
    <arcXML:unitPrice>765.00</arcXML:unitPrice>
    <arcXML:qty>35</arcXML:qty>
  </arcXML:line>
```

We seem to have that problem licked. Here's another common one: How would I put an angle bracket or an apostrophe into my XML document so that it is not interpreted as marking the opening of a tag or an attribute? The answer is that we use escape characters, known as *entity references*. The five common ones, and the characters they represent, are listed in Table 23-1.

Table 23-1. *Common XML Entity References*

Entity Reference	Character
&gt;	>
&lt;	<
&amp;	&
&apos;	'
&quot;	"

Anytime you need to use one of these characters in a normal part of the XML content, you should use the special entity reference, as in this example:

```
<comment>He said &quot;No comment&quot;</comment>
```

Don't forget the semicolon on the end. You can even build your own entity references to save work, much like an ABAP macro.

An extension of this facility is to use Unicode characters in your text. For example, copy the following code into an XML document:

```
<!-- Example of Unicode in Action -->
<arabic>&#1571;&#1607;&#1604;&#1575;&#1611;&#1576;
&#1603;&#1605;&#1601;&#1610;&#1616;&#1593;&#1575;&#1604;&#1605;</arabic>
```

Save the document as `name.xml` and open it with a web browser. You should see a result similar to Figure 23-1.

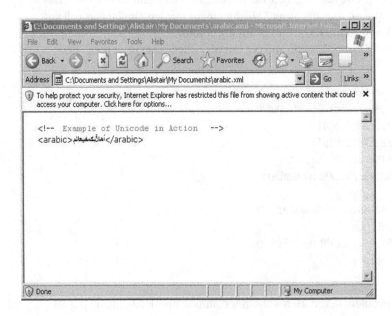

Figure 23-1. *Unicode displayed in XML*

We've discovered two very exciting things here! First, we can display Unicode characters in a standard browser, and second we can use our browser as a checker to see if our XML is correct or *well-formed*. Figure 23-2 shows what happens if our XML is not well-formed.

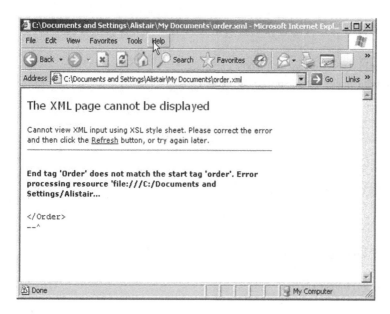

Figure 23-2. *Using the browser to check whether the XML is well-formed*

The error that I introduced was to remove a forward slash from one of the order elements, causing the check to fail. My document end was reached without finding the end of the order element.

At this point, you should do a few exercises with XML and use the browser or a specialized XML product to check whether your results are well-formed.

Parsing the XML Document

Although in the SAP environment you will rarely have to parse your own XML, it is important to know parsing so you can debug problems when they occur.

There are two main methods of parsing: using the SAX parser and using the DOM parser. In this section, we will be examining the SAX 2.0 parser. Free versions of this are widely available for Java. We are going to be using the Xerces version of the SAX 2.0 parser from Apache (http://www.apache.org). We could have chosen to use the one from Sun—they are very similar.

Please follow the installation instructions carefully. The latest version of the parser has changed, and there are now two JAR files to include in your CLASSPATH. These are xerxesImpl.jar and xml-apis.jar.

Let's first have a look at our main program, where we will call the SAX parser:

```
package arcParsing;

/**
 * @author Alistair
 *
 * All rights reserved by Alistair Rooney (c) 2005
 * Unless specifically waived under Open Source Agreement
 *
 * 09-Aug-2005
 */
import org.xml.sax.*;
import java.io.*;
import org.apache.xerces.parsers.*;
public class parseOrder
{

    public static void main(String[] args)
    {
        parseOrder po = new parseOrder();
        po.startP("C:\\order.xml");
    }
    public void startP(String xmlFile)
    {
        ContentHandler cont = new ContentHandling();
        try
        {
            XMLReader mySAX = new SAXParser();
            mySAX.setContentHandler(cont);
            mySAX.parse(xmlFile);
        }
        catch (IOException ioe)
        {
            System.out.println("IO Exception "+ioe.getMessage());
        }
        catch (SAXException se)
        {
            System.out.println("A SAX Exception has occurred "+se.getMessage());
        }


    }
}
```

As you probably know, it is very bad practice to instantiate a class from within itself, but this is just an illustration. Have a look at the main method. We create an instance of our own class, and then we call our method startP. We pass the XML file (in real life we would do this in a more elegant way) to the method. The method then instantiates a new parser and proceeds with parsing.

This is very simple, as you can see, but the best is yet to come. When we run the parser, it reads through our file and triggers events. All we have to do is handle those events. To do this, there is an interface that we can implement: the ContentHandler interface.

The ContentHandler Interface

As you can see in the code in the last section, we have created an instance of the ContentHandler:

```
ContentHandler cont = new ContentHandling();
```

ContentHandling is a class I wrote to implement the handler. There are eleven methods to implement in ContentHandler, which is a little long—I wrote an adapter class so we can use just the methods that we need. I have shown all of them to illustrate this fully, even though I do not have implementations for all of them. Here is the class:

```
package arcParsing;

/**
 * @author Alistair
 *
 * All rights reserved by Alistair Rooney (c) 2005
 * Unless specifically waived under Open Source Agreement
 *
 * 09-Aug-2005
 */
import org.xml.sax.*;
public class ContentHandling implements ContentHandler
{
    private Locator loc;

    public void setDocumentLocator(Locator locator)
    {
        this.loc = locator;
    }
    public void startDocument()throws SAXException
    {
        System.out.println("Parsing is Starting");
    }
    public void endDocument()throws SAXException
    {
        System.out.println("Parsing complete");
    }
    public void processingInstruction(String target, String data)throws SAXException
    {
        System.out.println("PI: Target="+target+" and Data="+data);
    }
```

```java
    public void startElement(String nmsURI, String localName,
               String qName, Attributes atts)
    {
       System.out.println("Start Element: Local Name="+localName);
       for(int i=0; i<atts.getLength(); i++)
       {
          System.out.println("Element has the attribute"
+atts.getLocalName(i)+" Value is "+atts.getValue(i));
       }
    }
    public void endElement(String nmsURI, String localName,
String qName)throws SAXException
    {
       System.out.println("End Element: Local Name="+localName);
    }
    public void characters(char[] ch, int start, int length)throws SAXException
    {
       String s = new String(ch, start, length);
       System.out.println("Characters="+s);
    }
    public void ignorableWhitespace(char[] ch, int start, int length)
    {
    // No implementation yet!
    }
    public void skippedEntity(String name)
    {
       System.out.println("Skipped Entity"+name);
    }
    public void startPrefixMapping(String prefix, String uri)
    {

    }
    public void endPrefixMapping(String prefix)
    {

    }
}
```

Each of these methods will be triggered when an event thrown by the parser is caught or handled. The setDocumentLocator method uses a Locator object to map the actual location within the XML file (column number, line number, etc.). This cannot be glossed over, as no callback will work without it. Notice the private variable loc. The startPrefixMapping and endPrefixMapping methods will report on our namespaces, if we have any.

The other methods are self-explanatory, so peruse the following output. Try to match the following results with the print statements in the program. Since this is a non-validating parser it will trigger the character method for the white space.

```
Parsing is Starting
Start Element: Local Name=order
Element has the attribute type Value is ZQ
Characters=

Start Element: Local Name=number
Characters=5072341
End Element: Local Name=number
Characters=

Start Element: Local Name=orderDate
Characters=20050801
End Element: Local Name=orderDate
Characters=

Start Element: Local Name=soldTo
Characters=14432
End Element: Local Name=soldTo
Characters=

Start Element: Local Name=shipTo
Characters=14476
End Element: Local Name=shipTo
Characters=

Start Element: Local Name=delDate
Characters=20050815
End Element: Local Name=delDate
Characters=

Start Element: Local Name=poNumber
Characters=90-6627-3
End Element: Local Name=poNumber
Characters=

Start Element: Local Name=line
Element has the attribute id Value is 010
Characters=

Start Element: Local Name=material
Characters=GI-72388
End Element: Local Name=material
Characters=
```

```
Start Element: Local Name=uom
Characters=ea
End Element: Local Name=uom
Characters=

Start Element: Local Name=unitPrice
Characters=765.00
End Element: Local Name=unitPrice
Characters=

Start Element: Local Name=qty
Characters=35
End Element: Local Name=qty
Characters=

End Element: Local Name=line
Characters=
Characters=

Start Element: Local Name=line
Element has the attribute id Value is 020
Characters=

Start Element: Local Name=material
Characters=GI-34490
End Element: Local Name=material
Characters=

Start Element: Local Name=uom
Characters=ea
End Element: Local Name=uom
Characters=

Start Element: Local Name=unitPrice
Characters=200.00
End Element: Local Name=unitPrice
Characters=

Start Element: Local Name=qty
Characters=76
End Element: Local Name=qty
Characters=

End Element: Local Name=line
Characters=
```

```
Start Element: Local Name=line
Element has the attribute id Value is 030
Characters=

Start Element: Local Name=material
Characters=GI-982254
End Element: Local Name=material
Characters=

Start Element: Local Name=uom
Characters=ea
End Element: Local Name=uom
Characters=

Start Element: Local Name=unitPrice
Characters=25.00
End Element: Local Name=unitPrice
Characters=

Start Element: Local Name=qty
Characters=12
End Element: Local Name=qty
Characters=

End Element: Local Name=line
Characters=

Start Element: Local Name=comment
Characters=Deliver at bay 3
End Element: Local Name=comment
Characters=

End Element: Local Name=order
Parsing complete
```

There are other handlers that you should be aware of in the SAX environment. The most important is the ErrorHandler. Review the API documentation that comes with the parser you choose to use.

Constraining the XML Document

XML is used in many areas these days. It can be used to hold configuration information, as we saw with servlets and JSP and it can be used in conjunction with XPATH or XSLT to change a single XML document and present it in many different ways. There are many interesting XML-based technologies out there at the moment, and more will be developed.

One of the really cool technologies is the Java Architecture for XML Binding (JAXB). You can download this set of APIs as part of the Java Web Services Developer Pack from Sun. What these APIs will do for you is examine an XML schema and actually build Java classes and interfaces for you. Apart from this being an exciting feature on its own, it will allow Java developers to use XML without in-depth knowledge of SAX, DOM, or XML schemas by treating schema-valid XML as a Java object! I encourage you to research it after you have read this lesson.

An interesting experiment is using Microsoft Office to create and open XML files. You will soon realize that you can transport files between Excel and Word using XML.

Incidentally, open an XML file with Word, and you will see something similar to Figure 23-3.

Figure 23-3. *Using Microsoft Word to view XML*

XML can also be used to transmit IDocs (SAP Intermediate Documents) and other forms of EDI documents between elements of a single business or between businesses. This is called business-to-business (B2B) communication. I can now send my well-formed XML file to my business partner, so that he can process my order.

Traditionally the interface developers from both companies would agree on an XML format for the document. For example, there will always be a line element, and the line element will always contain a material number. Once the two parties have agreed on this format, they have a mechanism to check whether the document is valid, meaning that it conforms to the agreed-upon rules.

There are several ways to represent this agreement, or contract. The two main ones are the Document Type Definition (DTD) and the schema.

Using DTDs

DTDs are documents that constrain the XML document. They use a special syntax with their own type definitions.

The ELEMENT Type Definition

Every element we use in an XML document must be declared in the DTD before it can be considered valid. If we had an atomic element—one that contains no child elements—and it contained normal character data, we could have an ELEMENT declaration like this:

```
<!ELEMENT orderDate (#PCDATA)>
```

Do you remember orderDate from the sales order XML example at the beginning of this lesson? What we have declared here is that we have an atomic element called orderDate, and that it contains normal character data.

What if we had child elements we needed to declare. Look at the following example. It's not too difficult to see what is happening here:

```
<!ELEMENT line (material, uom, unitPrice, qty)>
<!ELEMENT material (#PCDATA)>
<!ELEMENT uom (#PCDATA)>
<!ELEMENT unitPrice (#PCDATA)>
<!ELEMENT qty (#PCDATA)>
```

This tells the validating parser that I can have a line element. The line has no data itself, but it does contain four *child* elements: material, uom, unitPrice, and qty. Each of these can contain character data. What you have not seen here is that I have issued an invisible instruction to the validating parser—I have told it that there can be *only one* of each child element. If I tried to put in two uom elements, the file would not validate.

If I wanted *one or more* uom elements, I would use the + symbol, like so:

```
<!ELEMENT line (material, uom+, unitPrice, qty)>
```

Table 23-2 lists the symbols we can use.

Table 23-2. *Symbols Used in DTD Element Declarations*

Symbol	Description
(blank)	The element may only appear once.
?	The element may appear zero or one times.
+	The element may appear one or more times.
*	The element may appear zero or more times.
|	This means that one element *or* another may be used (but only one).

We could define our order line like this:

```
<!ELEMENT line (material, uom, unitPrice, qty|netWeight)>
```

This would indicate that we could use either the qty element or the netWeight element.

The ATTLIST Type Definition

Like the ELEMENT definition, the ATTLIST type definition specifies the attributes that are expected in the XML file. Let's examine the following XML snippet:

```
<order type="ZQ">
```

We would represent this as follows:

```
<!ELEMENT order (number, orderDate, soldTo, shipTo, delDate, poNumber, line)>
<!ATTLIST order type CDATA #REQUIRED>
```

We have defined our type attribute that belongs to the order element.

CDATA means that the attribute is character data—a string—and that is it required or mandatory. Instead of #REQUIRED, the attribute could also be #IMPLIED or #FIXED. #IMPLIED means that the attribute does not appear in the document, and #FIXED specifies a constant value.

There are other values other than CDATA. These fall into the tokenized and enumerated categories. In simple terms, CDATA can take any string data, whereas tokenized types can be lexically and semantically constrained, and enumerated types must take one of a list of values. These are worth researching further if you intend using DTD constraints often.

The DOCTYPE Type Definition

Once we have developed our DTD, we need to do one of two things:

- Include the DTD within our XML document.

- Have a reference in our XML document to point to an external DTD.

The usefulness of having an internally defined DTD is somewhat limited. The syntax is as follows:

```
<!DOCTYPE arcXML:order[
DTD code in here . . .
]>
```

External references are much more useful, and they increase in usefulness if you store them on the Web. You may even choose to use the "standard" XML formats suggested by the W3C organization.

The format for declaring an external (but not public) DTD is as follows:

```
<?xml version="1.0" standalone="no"?>
<!DOCTYPE arcXML:order SYSTEM "order.dtd">
```

This tells the parser to look for a DTD file on the system called order.dtd. To use a public DTD, we make use of the PUBLIC keyword. Here's an example:

```
<?xml version="1.0" standalone="no"?>
<!DOCTYPE arcXML:order PUBLIC "order.dtd" "http://www.rooney.co.za/xml/">
```

Although other DOCTYPE definitions are beyond the scope of this lesson, I thought I'd leave you with this example that you have probably seen before:

```
<!DOCTYPE HTML PUBLIC "-//W3C//DTD HTML 4.0 Transitional//EN">
```

It should be easy enough to follow.

Using Schemas

The subject of schemas has grown enormously since its official inception in 2001. Entire books have been written on the subject, so this section will simply give you the basic tools to extend your knowledge further.

DTDs existed before schemas, so why was a new method of constraint considered necessary? To answer this, we need to look at the shortcomings of the DTD. As we have seen, the DTD has its own syntax. Since the constraint document can be dynamic, it would be better to keep it as XML so that we can extend it or change it easily. The DTD has 10 data types whereas the schema has over 44.

Schemas solve the extensibility issue rather elegantly because they are XML documents. Since they too need to be constrained, they can have a DTD to do this. The other difference is that when a document that has been successfully validated against a schema, it is called *schema-valid*, and not just *valid*.

The Root Element

So, if our schema is an XML document, it must have a root element. We shall call ours schema. Notice the namespace declaration in bold in the following code:

```
<xsd:schema targetNamespace="http://localhost"
     xmlns="http://localhost"
     xmlns:xsd="http://www.w3.org/2001/XMLSchema"
     elementFormDefault="qualified">

</xsd:schema>
```

The namespace XSD (XML Schema Definition) points to the XMLSchema definition on the Web. The additional namespace declaration pointing to localhost is needed because we have our own XML files that should not be constrained by the XMLSchema definition on the Web.

The Element Declaration

Declaring elements in a schema is fairly straightforward. We do it like this:

```
<xsd:element name="orderDate" type="xsd:date" minOccurs="1" maxOccurs="1" />
```

There are a few things to note here, however. The first is that we have used the shorthand way of ending the tag. We could have used </xsd:element> instead. The second point is that we have actually declared the date as such, and not defaulted to a generic type (as we do in the DTD) but to a specific data type.

There are quite a few data types that we can use. They are separated into two separate groups: a few built-in types and as many user-defined types as we wish to create. Here are some of the most popular built-in types:

- `boolean`
- `date`
- `dateTime`
- `decimal`
- `double`
- `float`
- `gDay` (Gregorian day)
- `gMonth` (Gregorian month)
- `gYear` (Gregorian year)
- `string`
- `time`
- `byte`
- `short`
- `token` (a string with no white space)

Although you can see that we have `minOccurs` and `maxOccurs` statements in the line, these are superfluous in this case, as the default is that an element may only occur once. I have included them here for the sake of illustration only. They are self-explanatory. If you wished to make the upper limit infinite, you could do so by using this:

```
maxOccurs="unbounded"
```

Complex Types

In our sales order XML example at the start of the lesson, we had a number of child elements. We need to be able to represent these in our schema, and we do this by using the `complexType` tag.

Even though most developers will use complex types to show child elements, it can also be used to build special types that can be used in normal simple elements. I won't bore you with the details in this short introduction, but please research this if you intend to do a lot of work with schemas.

The best way to illustrate a complex type is with an example. First let's look at the XML code we want to define:

```
<arcXML:line id="010">
    <arcXML:material>GI-72388</arcXML:material>
    <arcXML:uom>ea</arcXML:uom>
    <arcXML:unitPrice>765.00</arcXML:unitPrice>
    <arcXML:qty>35</arcXML:qty>
</arcXML:line>
```

Remember this from our sales order? Now let's develop the schema for the preceding code:

```
<xsd:element name="material" type="xsd:string" />
<xsd:element name="uom" type="xsd:string" />
<xsd:element name="unitPrice" type="xsd:decimal" />
<xsd:element name="qty" type="xsd:decimal" />
<xsd:element name="line" maxOccurs="unbounded" >
  <xsd:complexType>
    <xsd:sequence>
      <xsd:element ref="material"/>
      <xsd:element ref="uom"/>
      <xsd:element ref="unitPrice"/>
      <xsd:element ref="qty"/>
    </xsd:sequence>
</xsd:complexType>
```

This may seem a little cryptic at first, but let's step through it. We have declared the elements before we declared the structure or complex type. The final element is the line element—you can see that line has child elements. Next, we declare our complex type and the sequence that they need to be in. We then use the element tag again to reference the previously declared elements. Although we can declare the elements inside the complex type, this method gives us greater flexibility.

If you examine the XML again, you will notice that we seem to have ignored something. Well, in fact we have. The attributes have not been defined.

Attribute Declaration

Declaring an attribute is really quite simple. Have a look at the following example:

```
<xsd:attribute name="id" type="xsd:integer" use="required"/>
```

Because we are experts in XML now, we can read this quite easily. The use addition tells the parser that this attribute is required. Incidentally, we can also have a default value. To do this, we use the default keyword, followed by the actual value, like so:

```
<xsd:attribute name="gpsSetting" type="xsd:boolean" default="false"/>
```

When we do this, the use keyword may not be used.

Let's close this lesson on XML by taking a look at this keyword in context:

```
<xsd:element name="material" type="xsd:string" />
<xsd:element name="uom" type="xsd:string" />
<xsd:element name="unitPrice" type="xsd:decimal" />
<xsd:element name="qty" type="xsd:decimal" />
<xsd:element name="line" maxOccurs="unbounded" >
<xsd:complexType>
   <xsd:sequence>
   <xsd:element ref="material"/>
   <xsd:element ref="uom"/>
   <xsd:element ref="unitPrice"/>
   <xsd:element ref="qty"/>
</xsd:sequence>
<xsd:attribute name="id" type="xsd:integer" use="required"/>
</xsd:complexType>
```

An important part of XML in the SAP environment is a subset known as SOAP. In the next lesson, we will explore Java Message Service and SOAP. If you use Exchange Infrastructure, this lesson is mandatory!

■■■

Java Messaging Services

If you have had experience of messaging middleware, like MQSeries from IBM, you will already understand the concept of messaging. There are many different forms of messaging—some use mailboxes (where a message must be placed in the mailbox and then retrieved from it), and some use direct connections.

Messaging can be broken down into two models: *synchronous* and *asynchronous*. Synchronous messaging requires that a response be received from the message recipient to say that the message was received in good order. Asynchronous messaging requires no such confirmation and for this reason can be less reliable. Asynchronous messaging is highly analogous to sending a letter. (When we cover SOAP, we will expand on this analogy.)

Java Message Service (JMS) is asynchronous, but it is highly reliable. This reliability can be "turned down" if you have an application that doesn't worry about missed or duplicate messages. JMS is also said to be *loosely coupled*; that is, it does not communicate directly with the other party.

Note The BAPI (RFC) call discussed in Lesson 20 was a good example of a *tightly coupled* system.

JMS is simply a collection of classes (APIs) that developers can use to send and receive messages. The standard format for these messages is XML—specifically the Simple Object Access Protocol (SOAP). This protocol is equally important in the SAP world, since Exchange Infrastructure makes use of JMS and uses SOAP/XML as its communications protocol.

Although JMS can adequately support both *point to point* messaging and *publish and subscribe* messaging, we will only be covering the former in this lesson.

THE TWO CONNECTION METHODOLOGIES

There are two ways to design your message connection. The first is to use a *point to point* connection. Essentially this relays a message from point A to point B and vice versa. This is still one of the most common implementations, but increasingly people are using *pub/sub* or *publish/subscribe*. In this case, the message is sent to a topic, and it can be used or "consumed" by many clients. In this lesson, we will be examining a point to point scenario.

It is important to keep in mind that JMS and SOAP are completely separate technologies. I am discussing them together here for the simple reason that we do not send messages using JMS in SAP without first putting the messages into a SOAP format. JMS does not *require* that your messages be in SOAP format, but it does make life easier. Conversely, SOAP (or SOAP with Attachments API for Java—SAAJ—from a Java perspective) works with countless other technologies outside the JMS context.

JMS Scenarios

Common messaging scenarios include sending intra-organizational messages and B2B (business-to-business) messages. Let's take a look at an example of a simple intra-organizational message, also called application-to-application (A2A) messages.

Let's assume we have an order entry application that allows for the creation of a sales order. Once the sales order has been created, we may want to send this information to a production system to produce the stock for the order. This is not a contrived example—many enterprises have separate systems for ordering and production. The production system will then feed this information into its demand planning, and it may send other messages to other systems, like accounting, using the same mechanism.

A common trend these days is to outsource aspects of the business that are not "core" to the enterprise. Let's say this company—Acme Beans—makes beans. It does not consider distribution of its product to be "core" to the company. It uses another company—ABC Logistics—to handle storage and distribution of the product.

Once a customer places an order, this must be communicated to the distributor, and the distributor must tell Acme Beans that the delivery has taken place. Figure 24-1 shows this in schematic form. This can be accomplished using JMS to send these documents as messages, providing a fast and reliable way of communicating across businesses.

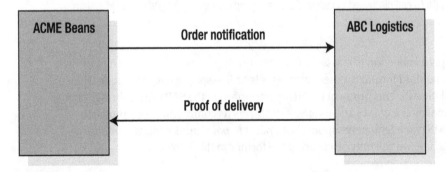

Figure 24-1. *A simple B2B process*

These days it is rare that JMS works by itself. It can, of course, but it is more efficient and more robust to have middleware between the two parties.

SOAP

Earlier in this lesson, I compared asynchronous communication to sending a letter. As we delve into SOAP, we can take this letter analogy a little further. Have a look at the diagram in Figure 24-2 to get an idea of this.

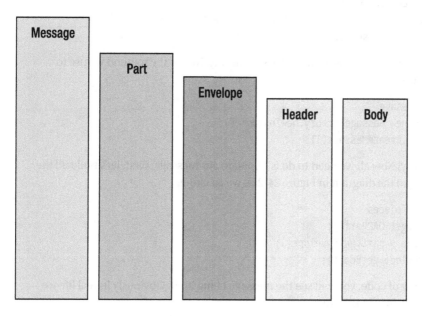

Figure 24-2. *The SOAP layer*

Think of Russian dolls when you look at this figure. The body and header live inside the envelope, the envelope lives inside the part, and the part is wrapped inside the message. The actual data in the message—an order, for example—will be contained in the body. The header, which is optional, will contain routing, level of service, intermediate destinations, and sending and receiving party information. The envelope will contain information about message encoding—this is a very powerful aspect of SOAP, as it allows us to create our own data types.

JAXM

Now that we have a basic understanding of the SOAP message, let's look at how we would code up a very simple example. Our example program will send a request for stock to another party and receive the response.

Since we are using Java to process our XML/SOAP messages, we should use Java API for XML Messaging (JAXM). JAXM implements SOAP with Attachments API for Java (SAAJ). You can download JAXM and SAAJ as separate APIs, or you can point your CLASSPATH to the JAR file for your J2EE implementation.

The packages we are primarily interested in are these:

```
javax.xml.soap
javax.xml.messaging
```

The first thing we need to do is build the connection. This must be done within a try . . . catch block.

```
try
    {
    // Create the connection first
    SOAPConnectionFactory scf = new SOAPConnectionFactory.newInstance();
    SOAPConnection con = scf.createConnection();
```

Now we need to create the message in a very similar way. Notice the method we use to create a new instance:

```
// Now create the message
MessageFactory mf = new MessageFactory.newInstance();
SOAPMessage msg = mf.createMessage();
```

It really is that easy! Now all we need to do is populate our message. First, let's build all the message pieces. Refer to the diagram in Figure 24-2 as we go along.

```
// Build the message pieces
SOAPPart part = msg.getSOAPPart();
SOAPEnvelope envelope = part.getEnvelope();
SOAPBody body = envelope.getBody();
```

In the next snippet of code, you will see the message being built. Obviously in real life we would not hard-code strings in this way:

```
// Create the SOAP request
Name bodyName = envelope.createName("request-stock", "Request
Stock","http://stock.acme.com");
SOAPBodyElement requestStock = body.addBodyElement(bodyName);
Name requestName = envelope.createName("request");
SOAPBodyElement request = requestStock.addChildElement(requestName);
request.addTextNode("Send Stock List");
msg.saveChanges();
```

Now we have our message. Next we need to create our target, or endpoint, and send the message through. Again, there are no surprises here. It isn't really necessary to save the changes using the saveChanges method, but we'll call it for safety's sake.

```
// Create Endpoint and send the request
URL endpoint = new URL("http://localhost:8080/stock/servlet/stocklist");
SOAPMessage response = con.call(msg, endpoint);
con.close();
// Quick and easy way to drill down to the body
SOAPBody responseBody = response.getSOAPBody();
// Old code
// SOAPBody responseBody = response.getSOAPPart().getEnvelope().getBody();
```

Note In the latest version of JAXM, we don't have to go through the part and envelope to get to the body and examine the response.

It may be confusing in the first part of the snippet to see a `response` when we are trying to *send* the message, but let's look at each line. The URL sets up the `endpoint`. You can probably see here that we are calling a servlet to send a `response`. In the next line, we run the `call` method, sending the message and the destination as arguments.

We now wait until a `response` has been sent. Once we have the `response`, we would normally iterate through the elements, examining the data.

Other Considerations When Using JMS

Although the previous somewhat trivial example will work without any problems, many enterprises insist on a certain level of guarantee that messages are transmitted successfully. For this reason, we normally employ middleware to manage our connections in a more professional way.

If you are working in an IBM WebSphere environment, for example, you would probably use MQSeries to manage your messaging. In this case, you would use the APIs provided by IBM to build your connection.

The same argument applies to a SAP Exchange Infrastructure environment. For the point to point model, you would use the `javax.jms.QueueSender` class to send messages to a queue, and the `javax.jms.QueueReceiver` class to retrieve messages. The publish/subscribe model also has its own SAP-specific APIs. These are `javax.jms.Topic` to set up a topic, `javax.jms.TopicPublisher` to send to a topic, and `javax.jms.TopicSubscriber` to consume a message.

In short, when working in specific environments, you should review the APIs first.

In the next lesson, we will look at messaging again, in something called a message-driven bean. This is all part of the wonderful world of Enterprise JavaBeans.

■■■

Enterprise JavaBeans 3.0

One of the biggest complaints in the Java community recently has been the increasing complexity of the J2EE environment. This has been especially valid in the area of Enterprise JavaBeans (EJB). EJB was not easy to use in the 1.1 environment, and although version 2.0 introduced some additional functionality—like message-driven beans—it did little towards reducing the complexity of developing with EJB.

Well, I have good news, and I have bad news. The good news is that the latest release of EJB (version 3.0) has made a good attempt at reducing this complexity. The bad news is that I will go through the older specification first. I do this so that you can see how EJB has developed. This, I hope, will make you a better practitioner of EJB.

Working with EJB 2.x

EJB allows for a distributed implementation of a Java application. The implementation, or bean, is wrapped inside a container, which manages the security, the transactions, and the persistence of each operation. A container can be likened to a web server running a servlet. Many beans can run in one container.

There are basically three different types of beans: the session bean, the entity bean, and the message-driven bean.

The Session Bean

It is useful to think of a session bean as representing a client session. Although this is not strictly true, it's a good enough analogy. The session bean works for the client, allowing the client to run its methods. It hides the complexity from the client.

A session bean "belongs" to one client. When the client terminates, the session bean is no longer associated with that client.

There are some rules for building a session bean:

- The bean must implement the SessionBean interface

- The class must be `public`

- The class cannot be `abstract` or `final`

- The class must implement at least one `ejbCreate` method

- The class should implement the business methods (more on this later)

- The class should contain a `public` constructor with no parameters

- It must not define the `finalize` method

Session beans themselves can be of two types: stateless and stateful.

Stateless Beans

Stateless beans receive messages from the client and send a returning messages. In other words, the bean does not stay connected to the client. Once the method call is complete, the connection between the client and the session bean is broken.

The benefits of using stateless beans are that they are held in memory, not on disk, and as such they have a performance benefit over stateful beans. They can also service many clients (though only one at a time) and they can also implement a web service.

Stateful Beans

In contrast to the stateless bean, the stateful bean retains a connection to the client. This is more like making a telephone call than sending a message. Because of this, the state that exists between the client and the bean is called the *conversational state*.

You would use a stateful session bean if you need to retain information about the client from one invocation to the next. It is also useful to act as a *façade controller* to manage entity beans.

The Entity Bean

The entity bean represents a business object. This is held in a persistent state (on storage somewhere). A good example of an entity bean would be the object for a sales order. This would typically read and write sales order information to the database.

If the bean itself is writing to and reading from the database, it is called *bean-managed* persistence. If the container manages the persistence, then the entity bean does not need to code for it—the EJB container itself makes the calls to the database. This is called *container-managed* persistence.

The entity bean must use some code called EJB Query Language (QL) to tell the container what to read or write from the database. This is actually a nice way of doing things, since the entity bean does not need to worry about the underlying database, database drivers, and the like.

Here is a snippet showing some EJB QL:

```
SELECT OBJECT(p)
FROM Player p
WHERE p.teams IS NOT EMPTY
```

Many clients can use an entity bean, since many clients may want to update the same data. This is managed by working within transactions. The transaction management is handled by the EJB container.

Each entity bean must have a *primary key*, just as each database record needs a key—it needs this to be uniquely identified. Also, like database records, entity beans can have relationships. For example, our sales order entity bean would have a *relationship* to the customer entity bean.

Obviously, if you have written your own database code in the bean, you would have to manage your own relationships. However, if you have used EJB QL to determine the relationships, the container will manage them.

If you have chosen to let the EJB container manage your relationships, you must use the Abstract schema to describe these. The Abstract schema is then referenced in the *deployment descriptor*, which is an XML file. Don't worry too much about the deployment descriptor—this gets easier in EJB 3.0.

Remember that the entity bean is best used for *business entities* like sales orders, and not for *processes* like checking stock.

The Message-Driven Bean

The message-driven bean (MDB) is very like a Listener class (discussed in Lesson 17), but this type of bean waits for messages from JMS. These messages can be sent from anywhere; hence the beauty of the message-driven bean. You can probably see how this could be scaled up in a very easy—and robust—way.

MDBs are very similar to stateless session beans. Remember the letter analogy? The MDB retains no data linked to a client. A single MDB can also service many clients, and you can also have a "pool" of MDBs, which the EJB container will assign to clients.

One of the main differences between MDBs and stateless session beans, however, is how the client talks to the MDB. Instead of *directly* invoking the bean, it relies on its message to *trigger* the running of the bean.

The bean will implement the MessageListener interface. This means that when a message arrives, it will trigger the onMessage method to process the message. In turn, this method will probably use other beans—because we want some healthy delegation in our design—and these would be session or entity beans, or both.

Figure 25-1 shows this relationship.

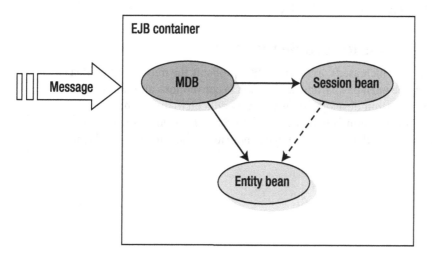

Figure 25-1. *Invocation of a message-driven bean*

EJB Clients

Now that we've seen the three basic bean types, let's examine clients in a little more detail. Essentially there are two types of clients: local and remote.

- Local clients are clients that run on the same Java Virtual Machine (JVM) as the bean.

- Remote clients can be anywhere, and could be a web service or even another bean.

We will see some practical application of these types of clients later in the lesson.

Components in a 2.x EJB Scenario

Next we'll examine the *old* components of the EJB. Remember that this has changed substantially in 3.0, which I will cover later.

There are several types of components you should be aware of:

- **Deployment descriptor:** This is an XML file that contains information about the bean, such as its persistence type. NetWeaver Developer Studio will assist you in the creation of this file, and Sun has its own wizard called deploytool. Occasionally you may have to edit this file manually.

- **The bean class:** We will, of course, go into more detail on this later, but suffice it to say that it is the class to hold the business logic.

- **Remote and local interfaces:** Web services require their own interfaces.

- **Helper or utility classes:** These are also included as components.

Once we have all these components, we can "wrap them to go." We use something similar to a JAR file to do this. In effect, it is an EJB JAR file, but you will see this more commonly referred to as an EAR, or Enterprise Archive, file.

Naming Conventions for EJB Beans

We are entering an area of increased complexity (EJB is probably the most complex area of Java development), so we must pay particular attention to conventions and standards. If we don't stick to a convention, our development will be very difficult to maintain.

Table 25-1 shows the recommended standards from Sun. I have no reason to differ from their suggestions. The letters *DD* in the table denote items that are in the deployment descriptor.

Table 25-1. *Sun Naming Conventions for EJB Beans*

Item	Syntax	Example
Enterprise bean name (DD)	`<name>Bean`	`AccountBean`
EJB JAR display name (DD)	`<name>JAR`	`AccountJAR`
Enterprise bean class	`<name>Bean`	`AccountBean`
Home interface	`<name>Home`	`AccountHome`
Remote interface	`<name>`	`Account`
Local home interface	`<name>LocalHome`	`AccountLocalHome`
Local interface	`<name>Local`	`AccountLocal`
Abstract schema (DD)	`<name>`	`Account`

█Note Remember that EJB 3.0 reduces much of this complexity, so please don't give up yet. We will cover 3.0 soon.

Creating a Simple EJB 2.x Project

Now that we have got the background on EJB 2.x, we can look at building a small EJB 2.x example: an adaptation of the SAP calculator example provided with NWDS. This example will be presented in a series of steps, which can easily be followed without much thought, but please make the effort to understand exactly what we are doing.

The first thing we need to do after starting NetWeaver Developer Studio is create an EJB project:

1. Select File ➤ New ➤ EJB Module Project as shown in Figure 25-2. Call your project CalculatorEJB.

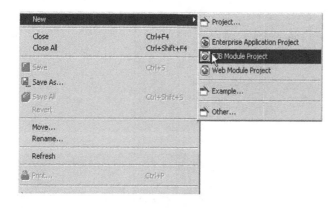

Figure 25-2. *Creating a new EJB project*

2. In the J2EE Explorer, click on the Project node, and right-click to create a new EJB as shown in Figure 25-3. Call it Calculator, and make it a stateless session bean.

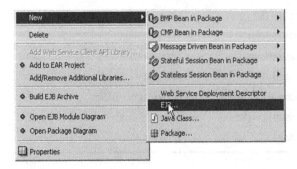

Figure 25-3. *Creating a new EJB*

3. Give it a meaningful package name. Click Next and accept the default names given. Click Next again.

4. In the business methods screen shown in Figure 25-4 you can create the business methods of the bean. Click the Add button to add a method.

Figure 25-4. *Creating EJB methods*

5. We are going to build a simple calculator, so we will need methods to do basic math. Add four methods, for add, subtract, divide, and multiply. Use floats for the two incoming parameters and a float for the return parameter, as shown in Figure 25-5.

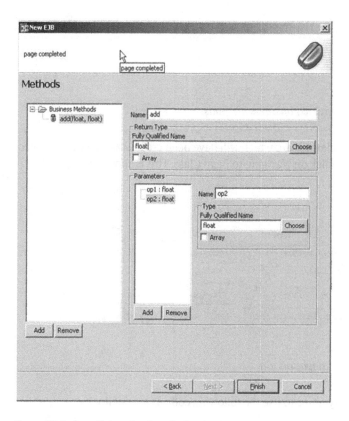

Figure 25-5. *Specifying the details for the business methods*

6. Click the Finish button when you're done. You should see the newly created Java files in the calculator package, as shown in Figure 25-6.

Figure 25-6. *Automatically created Java files*

7. You will also see the methods under ejb-jar.xml, as shown in Figure 25-7.

Figure 25-7. *The newly created business methods*

8. Double-click on CalculatorBean, which will have been created as part of the project, and in the right pane click on Navigate to Bean Class. This is shown in Figure 25-8.

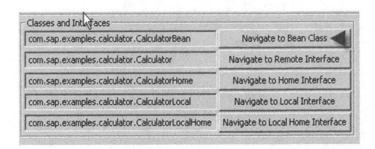

Figure 25-8. *Using the navigation aid*

9. Code the functionality. You can use the following code as a guideline:

```
    /**
  * Business Method.
  */
 public float add(float f1, float f2)
 {
    return f1 + f2;
 }


 /**
  * Business Method.
  */
 public float divide(float f1, float f2)
 {
     return f1 / f2;
 }
```

```
/**
 * Business Method.
 */
public float subtract(float f1, float f2)
{

    return f1-f2;
}


/**
 * Business Method.
 */
public float multiply(float f1, float f2)
{

    return f1*f2;
}
```

10. Save everything. This will automatically compile your code.

11. Create the archive by right-clicking on the CalculatorEJB module and choosing Build EJB Archive. This is shown in Figure 25-9.

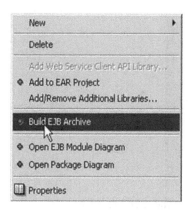

Figure 25-9. *Building an archive*

Our bean is created! Well, it's the bare bones, at least. It's a little naked, so we will now build a web project that will act as our "view." Follow these steps:

1. Create a new Web Module Project, and call it CalculatorWeb.

2. Now we want a bean (a normal one) and a JSP page to display it. Right-click on CalculatorWeb and create a Java class, as shown in Figure 25-10.

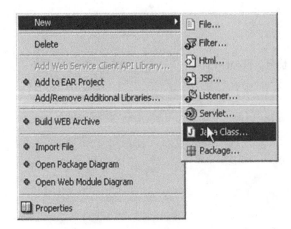

Figure 25-10. *Adding the Java bean*

3. Call the bean CalcProxy, and write code similar to the following:

```
/*
 * Created on Sep 14, 2005
 *
 * To change the template for this generated file go to
 * Window&gt;Preferences&gt;Java&gt;Code Generation&gt;Code and Comments
 */
package com.sap.examples.calculator.beans;

import javax.naming.InitialContext;
import javax.rmi.PortableRemoteObject;

import com.sap.examples.calculator.Calculator;
import com.sap.examples.calculator.CalculatorHome;

/**
 * @author arooney
 *
 * To change the template for this generated type comment go to
 * Window&gt;Preferences&gt;Java&gt;Code Generation&gt;Code and Comments
 */
public class CalcProxy
{
   private Calculator calc;
   public CalcProxy() throws Exception
   {
      init();
   }
```

```java
public void init() throws Exception
{
   //Lookup the enterprise bean
   try
   {
      InitialContext ctx = new InitialContext();
      Object ob = ctx.lookup("java:comp/env/ejb/CalculatorBean");
      CalculatorHome home = ( CalculatorHome )
PortableRemoteObject.narrow( ob, CalculatorHome.class );
 //Initialize the enterprise bean
      calc = home.create();
   } catch ( Exception e )
   {
      throw new Exception("Error instantiating Calculator EJB" +
e.toString());
   }


   }
public float getResult( String firstNumber, String secondNumber,
String expression ) throws Exception
{
   float result = 0;
   try
   {
     if ( firstNumber != null && secondNumber != null )
     {
      //Parse the input parameters
      float first = Float.parseFloat( firstNumber );
      float second = Float.parseFloat( secondNumber );
      int expr = Integer.parseInt( expression );

      //Invoke the relevant method of the enterprise bean
      switch ( expr )
      {
      case 1:
      result = calc.multiply( first, second );
      break;
      case 2:
      result = calc.divide( first, second );
      break;
      case 3:
      result = calc.add( first, second );
      break;
      case 4:
      result = calc.subtract( first, second );
      break;
      }
    }
```

```
        }catch (Exception re)
        {

            throw new Exception("Fill in all required fields with appropriate
➥values!");

        }
//Return the result of the calculation
        return result;

        }

}
```

That's the bean done. Now let's build the JSP page:

1. Add a JSP file as shown in Figure 25-11.

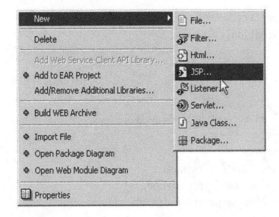

Figure 25-11. *Creating a JSP file*

2. Call it Calculator, and add code similar to the following:

```
<%@ page language="java" %>
<jsp:useBean id= "calc" scope= "session"    class=
"com.sap.examples.calculator.beans.CalcProxy" />

<html>
<head>
<title>
Calculator
</title>
<h1>Calculator Example</h1>
</head>
<body>
```

```
<FORM METHOD= "post" ACTION= "Calculator.jsp" >
<P> Select Operation: </P>
<P><SELECT NAME= "expression" >
<OPTION VALUE=1> Multiply
<OPTION VALUE=2> Divide
<option VALUE=3> Add
<option VALUE=4> Subtract
</SELECT></P>
<P> First number: </P>
<P><INPUT NAME= "firstnumber" size=10></P>
<P> Second number: </P>
<P><INPUT name= "secondnumber" size=10></P>
<P><INPUT TYPE= "SUBMIT" NAME= "Submit" VALUE= "Calculate" ></P>
</FORM>

<P>
<HR HEIGHT= "1px" WIDTH= "80%" COLOR= "#000000" >
</P>
<% try { %>
<P>
<B> <%="Result is " + calc.getResult(request.getParameter("firstnumber"),
 request.getParameter("secondnumber"),
➥request.getParameter("expression"))%></B>
</P>
<% } catch (Exception ex) { %>
    <%=ex.getMessage() %>
<% } %>

</body>
</html>
```

This should give you a screen like the one shown in Figure 25-12, but feel free to play around with the code to make it pretty!

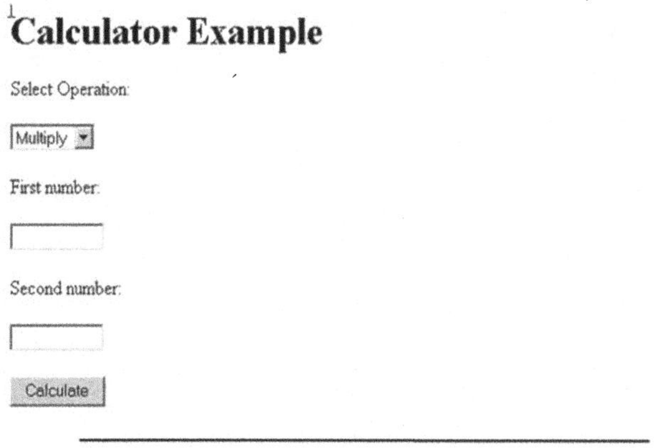

Calculator Example

Select Operation:

Multiply ▾

First number:

Second number:

Calculate

Figure 25-12. *The JSP preview window*

Now we need to create a web archive and link it to our EJB archive:

1. Double-click on the web.xml file and click on the EJB tab. You should see something like Figure 25-13.

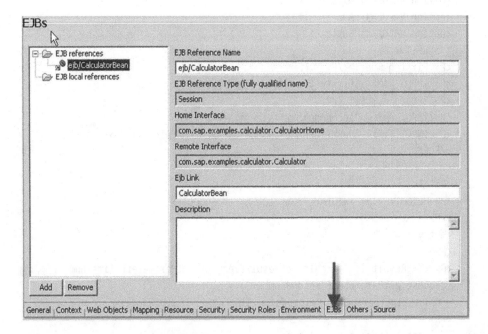

Figure 25-13. *Setting the* web.xml *file*

2. Make sure you have captured the EJB reference name and link, as shown in Figure 25-13. Now build the web archive by right-clicking the Calculator web project and choosing Build Web Archive, as shown in Figure 25-14. The web archive (WAR) file will contain all the elements that NetWeaver will need to run the web programs for the project.

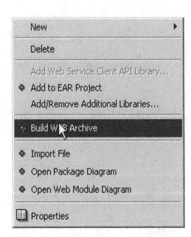

Figure 25-14. *Building the WAR file*

Now we need an EAR (Enterprise Archive) project to bind this all together:

1. Click on File ➤ New and choose Enterprise Application Project to create a new EAR, as shown in Figure 25-15.

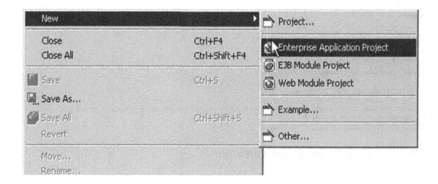

Figure 25-15. *Building the Enterprise Application Project*

2. Name it CalculatorEAR, and click Next.

3. Use CalculatorWeb and CalculatorEjb as reference projects. Click Finish.

4. Double-click on `application.xml` in the EAR project.

5. In the Modules tab, click on `CalculatorWeb.war` and enter **/Calculator** as the Context Root, as shown in Figure 26-16.

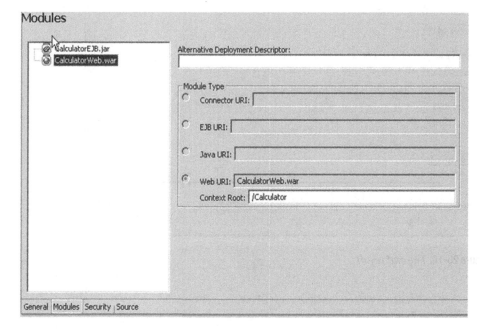

Figure 25-16. *Setting the* `application.xml`

6. Now build the EAR by right-clicking on the EAR project and selecting Build Application Archive, as shown in Figure 25-17.

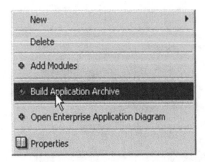

Figure 25-17. *Creating the application archive*

Now you are done! Ensure the SAP J2EE is running, and key the following into your favorite browser: http://localhost:50000/Calculator/Calculator.jsp. You should see the calculator in your browser, as in Figure 25-18. Have fun!

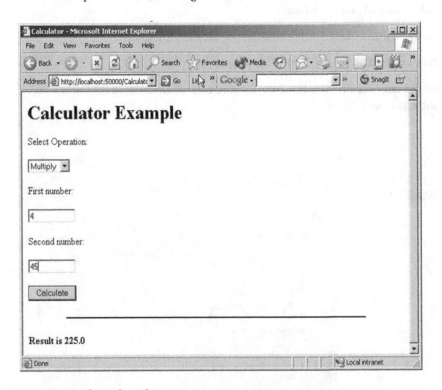

Figure 25-18. *The end result*

What's New in EJB 3.0?

The best thing about Enterprise Java 5 is that it tries to break down the complexity that has crept in over the last few years. As developers, we should worry about the problems we're solving and not the mechanism we use to code our solution.

In EJB 2.x we had to code all of the following, just for the session bean:

- A home interface that can be accessed by a remote client, and that defines the lifecycle methods for the session bean

- A remote interface that can be accessed by a remote client, and that defines the business methods for the session bean

- A bean class that contains the implementations of the home and remote interfaces

- A deployment descriptor (XML file) that specifies information about the bean, such as its name and type

Now, to create a stateless session bean using EJB 3.0, one simply needs to code the following:

- A bean class (properly annotated)

- A business interface, which can be generated by default

In this regard, the EJB 3.0 specification has simplified a great deal of the non-problem-related complexity. There are two ways this has been done. The first is to exploit the new annotations specification in JDK 1.5 (now called Java 5), and the second is to use *plain old Java objects*, now called POJOs—no, I'm not joking.

Enterprise Java 5 started shipping in early 2006.

Annotations

Annotations take advantage of lessons learnt with XDoclet, a successful open source project. We can now use these annotations to start coding our configuration options and metadata directly into our beans. This effectively does away with the need for unwieldy XML deployment descriptors!

POJO Services

In the EJB 3.0 programming model, the old component model (the Home interfaces, the required deployment descriptors) is *out*. The new EJB beans and service objects are simply container-managed POJOs. But without a component model, how can the container manage those POJOs? In EJB 3.0, the interaction between the POJO class and the container is specified using *Java annotations*.

Developing an EJB 3.0 Session Bean

Once again, we will code a very simple "Hello World" EJB bean. We will need three Java programs:

- HelloLocal for the local interface
- HelloBean for the stateless session bean
- HelloServlet for the servlet

HelloLocal.java

This is the code for the interface.

```
package com.alistair.ejb;

public interface HelloLocal
{
  public String shoutOut();
}
```

Simple enough. The shoutOut method will be our business method.

HelloBean.java

This is the code for the bean. Notice the annotations—they are in bold to distinguish them from the normal code.

```
package com.alistair.ejb;

import javax.ejb.*;
import static javax.ejb.TransactionAttributeType.SUPPORTS;

@Stateless
public class HelloBean implements HelloLocal
{
  private String shout = "Not initialized";

  @Inject
  public void setShout(String shout)
  {
    this.shout = shout;
  }

  @TransactionAttribute(SUPPORTS)
  public String shoutOut()
  {
    return shout;
  }
}
```

Everything seems familiar here except for the annotations. Let's examine each of them in more detail:

- @Stateless tells our bean that it is a stateless session bean. This does many things for us, including creating a stub.

- @Inject will look up the shout string for us using Java Naming and Directory Interface (JNDI). This would be set up in the Web.xml file as an <env-entry>, like this:

```
<env-entry env-entry-name="shout"
           env-entry-type="java.lang.String"
           env-entry-value="Hello NetWeaver Peeps"/>
```

- @TransactionAttribute configures how transactions are managed. In HelloBean.java we don't care if we reuse an existing transaction, so we use the SUPPORTS keyword. Using the REQUIRED keyword would tell the container to start a new transaction.

HelloServlet.java

Now we can examine the client. In this example, the client is a servlet. And once again, the annotation is in bold.

```java
package com.alistairrooney.ejb;

import java.io.*;
import javax.servlet.*;
import javax.servlet.http.*;
import javax.ejb.EJB;

public class HelloServlet extends GenericServlet
{
  private HelloLocal hello;

  @EJB(name="HelloBean")
  public void setHello(HelloLocal hello)
  {
    this.hello = hello;
  }

  public void service(HttpServletRequest req, HttpServletResponse res)
    throws IOException, ServletException
  {
    PrintWriter out = res.getWriter();
    if (hello == null)
    {
      out.println("This example requires JDK 1.5");
      return;
    }
```

```
    out.println(hello.shoutOut());
  }
}
```

The @EJB notation tells the container to look up the HelloBean session bean. We could have added this to our web.xml file, but this is so much more elegant.

Honestly that's it! Yes, you will have to configure your server. SAP J2EE does not support EJB 3.0 as I write this, but since SAP is very much part of the Java Community Process, we can expect to see this remedied shortly.

Developing an EJB 3.0 Entity Bean

Now that we have had a look at a simple example, let's explore developing an entity bean. I'm going to use the good old employee object here, but I'm only going to provide code snippets. If you really want to code this example, you will have to fill in the blanks.

The Entity Bean

```
@Entity
@Table(name = "EMP")
public class Employee implements Serializable
{
  private int empNo;
  private String eName;
  private double sal;

  @Id
  @Column(name="EMPNO", primaryKey=true)
  public int getEmpNo()
  {
    return empNo;
  }
// More code here
}
```

I think you can probably already start to see what is happening here. The @Entity annotation tells us that this is an entity bean, and the @Table tells us that we will be using the EMP table in our database.

The @Id annotation tells the compiler to use the integer empNo as the key. @Column makes sure we use column EMPNO in the table as our primary key.

The Session Bean

Now let's have a look at our session bean.

```
@Stateless
public class EmployeeFacadeBean implements EmployeeFacade
{
  @Resource
  private EntityManager em;
  private Employee emp;

  public Employee findEmployeeByEmpNo(int empNo)
  {
    return ((Employee) em.find("Employee",empNo));
  }

  public void addEmployee(int empNo, String eName, double sal)
  {
    if (emp == null)
    {
      emp = new Employee();
    }

    . . .

    em.persist(emp);
  }

  . . .

}
```

Here we have used the EntityManager API (`javax.persistence.EntityManager`) to create and find `Employee` objects.

The `@Resource` annotation is specifying that we have dependant objects, which will be "injected" (Sun's term) into the object persistence.

I think it's clear how much simpler it is coding EJB 3.0. We do have a problem, though. Currently in SAP we can only use the EJB 2.1 specification. However, this will change with further releases of NetWeaver.

Conclusion

Java is not a static language. If you think you can learn any language and then use that as your meal ticket for the next ten years, you are deluding yourself. Even ABAP has changed its face considerably over the last ten years.

It is our duty to continually research the new additions and changes to the languages we use to develop our applications. This is one of the exciting things about Java—it will always be changing.

Mr. Agassi, the CTO of SAP AG, has said (at SAP TechEd, in Boston, 2005) that Enterprise Services Architecture is the future, and that traditional IT is dead. Java is the grease that will oil the wheels of this new paradigm, so have fun with it!

Index

You Need the Companion eBook

Your purchase of this book entitles you to its companion eBook for only $10.

We believe this Apress title will prove so indispensable that you'll want to carry it with you everywhere, which is why we are offering the companion eBook for $10 to customers who purchase this book now. Convenient and fully searchable, the eBook version of any content-rich, page-heavy Apress book makes a valuable addition to your programming library. You can easily find, copy, and apply code—and then perform examples by quickly toggling between instructions and the application. Even simultaneously tackling a donut, diet soda, and complex code becomes simplified with hands-free eBooks!

Once you purchase this book, getting the $10 companion eBook is simple:

➊ Visit **www.apress.com/promo/tendollars/**.

➋ Complete a basic registration form to receive a randomly generated question about this title.

➌ Answer the question correctly in 60 seconds and you will receive a promotional code to redeem for the $10 eBook.

2560 Ninth Street • Suite 219 • Berkeley, CA 94710

Offer valid through 9/18/07.

Printed in the United States
By Bookmasters